"An essential read, providing the latest thinking and a practical guide for leaders who need to succeed and unlock the full potential of working in a matrix organization. Nurtured by the latest behavioral research, real cases, and proven techniques, the reader acquires new skills and strategies for growth and success in the matrix."

—Pedro Padierna-Bartning, retired chairman, PepsiCo-México

"Due to their deep familiarity with the subject and privileged position when openly talking with thousands of executives from all over the world about the challenge of succeeding in a matrix organization, John and Marty were able to grant us with an amazing set of tools to efficiently navigate in matrix organizations, securing we know what to do and, most important, HOW TO do it! It's a must-read book for anyone who deals with complex organizations."

—André Machado Fonseca, president, QMC Telecom do Brasil

"Whether you are in a private equity turnaround or a global corporation, this book provides a road map for transforming your company. Marty and John provide simple, practical tools that apply to any executive looking to maximize the effectiveness of their matrixed environment."

—Dan Guill, president and chief operating officer, Enlivant

"Collaboration and leading in a global matrix organization are two critical success factors and the new normal for leaders to be successful in today's fluid and dynamic business world. Marty and John combine both art and science into a practical portfolio of insights, skills development, and learning to help leaders successfully navigate the waters of the global matrix while developing and amplifying their leadership capabilities."

—Steve Milovich, former senior vice president of human resources, The Walt Disney Company

"In today's global business environment where organizations are increasingly integrated, the ability to collaborate across boundaries and influence without authority is critical. This is a no-nonsense book and a survival guide for executives looking to thrive in a global matrix."

—Steve Williams, CEO, PepsiCo Foods North America

"This book is a must-read for leaders in any industry. John and Marty bring so much knowledge and insight to the table—including how to navigate a variety

## Praise for *Leading in the Global Matrix*

"It's usually not difficult to explain the need for the shift to a matrix organization design. But it is certainly tough to explain what's needed to make it operate effectively—until now. This book delivers a practical explanation of why these structures often fail and clear guidance on the skills and attributes it takes to make them work. It's a must-read for leaders in today's global environment."

—Peter Gibbons, CEO, TireHub

"The world of business is experiencing unprecedented change and companies are using new organizational models to manage that change. Marty and John have a proven track record of success coaching thousands of successful executives. This book conveys all their tips in a practical and accessible way from building a network to effectively coping with organizational politics. It is a must-read for any aspiring leader seeking to jumpshift their effectiveness."

—Michael White, former CEO, DIRECTV

"*Leading in the Global Matrix* is more than a must-read business book. It proves the value of the matrix and gives leaders an inspiring and actionable road map to transform leadership, collaboration, and innovation in the modern world of work.

—Amy Thompson, executive vice president and chief people officer, Mattel, Inc.

"Organizations have always been complicated to navigate, even for the most savvy leaders. But in this new world where once traditional hierarchies are now more global, more interdependent, and more matrixed, reading this book is mandatory for any leader who wants to succeed. Leaders who avoid this wisdom do so at their peril."

—Michael Feiner, author, *The Feiner Points of Leadership*, Columbia Business School professor, and former senior executive, PepsiCo

"The gold standard of what it really takes to lead in global matrix organization . . . and oh-so practical!"

—Ed Betof, Ed.D., senior fellow in human capital, The Conference Board, and former WW VP of Talent Management and chief learning officer, BD of stakeholders in a fast-paced environment. This book is full of practical, easy-to-use advice that even the busiest leader can use."

—Candi Carter, executive producer, *The View*

"Leading in the matrix is complicated but necessary for all those that aim to succeed in the modern business arena. This book breaks it down in an easy-to-learn and practical fashion which will unlock value for all who read it."

—Josh Craver, head of talent management, FIS Global

"A must-read for anyone working in an organization, large or small. *Leading in the Global Matrix* is the first book that not only describes what a matrix is but also gives real, practical tips on how to manage and succeed in today's dynamic business world. John and Marty have taken the intimidation away from the concept of a matrix environment. This book is easy to read and touches on all the brilliant aspects John and Marty have been teaching for years. It's the answer we've all been looking for!"

—Dianne DeSevo, global chief HR officer, Engine Group

"As the pace of change in the marketplace accelerates, organizations are becoming more dynamic, agile, and matrixed—leaving career paths and organizations more challenging to navigate. With their unique perspective as 'inspirational pragmatists,' the authors provide a compelling guide to increasing effectiveness, career development, and personal growth that demystifies the art of leading in the matrix and renders it practical and immediately actionable."

—Brady Brewer, senior vice president of digital customer experience, Starbucks Coffee Company

"This book is a must-read. Seldman and Futterknecht assertively address the unspoken dimensions of a matrix organization by providing the correct skills and strategies to make it successful."

—Paula Santilli, CEO, PepsiCo Latin America and coauthor of *El Poder de Poder: Mujeres Construyendo Latinoamérica*

"Futterknecht and Seldman address the elephant in the room: the complexity within a matrix organization. Collaboration, respect, curiosity, and all the other attributes they analyze are spot-on to make the matrix work."

—Monica Bauer, vice president of corporate affairs, PepsiCo Latin America and coauthor of *El Poder de Poder: Mujeres Construyendo Latinoamérica*

"John is the expert in helping leaders navigate and thrive in matrixed organizations. He has distilled his extensive experiences in coaching leaders and working with global organizations into highly practical advice and tips that leaders at all levels can pick up and use. The strength of John's approach lies in addressing both the mindset and skill set for matrix success. And the skills really stick! Whether you are a leader undertaking an operating model transformation or looking to optimize the effectiveness of your matrix organization or a leader grappling with the challenges of leading within a new matrix, this book is for you. "

—Paula Coughlin, chief HR officer, Dixons Carphone, London

"This book isn't for corporations alone. Even the challenges our planet faces today cannot be solved without collaborating beyond borders, across the global 'matrix.' Whatever your chosen field, this book provides simple yet powerful tools to step change your effectiveness and impact at every level—your company, your community, your country, and our world."

—Sanjeev Chadra, former Chairman and CEO,
PepsiCo Asia, Middle East, and North Africa

"*Leading in the Global Matrix* is a much-needed road map for leaders and aspiring leaders to gain guidance and valuable tools to effectively navigate an increasingly complex world of work while leveraging high impact communication, collaboration, and influencing skills to advance organizational and individual success. This book should be required reading for all leadership and management development programs—both in academic and corporate university settings. The guidance offered is nothing short of game-changing!"

—Jovita Thomas-Williams, SPHR, GPHR, senior vice president
of human resources, Massachusetts General Hospital and
Massachusetts General Physicians Organization

"Every manager in matrix organizations can benefit from this book. My recommendation: read it, share it with others who are part of your matrix, and then discuss it together. You are certain to raise your game."

—Ed Bernard, senior advisor and retired vice chairman, T. Rowe Price

# LEADING IN THE GLOBAL MATRIX

## Proven Skills & Strategies to Succeed in a Collaborative World

John Futterknecht and
Marty Seldman

BenBella Books, Inc.
Dallas, TX

BenBella Books, Inc.
10440 N. Central Expressway, Suite 800
Dallas, TX 75231
www.benbellabooks.com
Send feedback to feedback@benbellabooks.com

Printed in the United States of America
10 9 8 7 6 5 4 3 2 1

Library of Congress Cataloging-in-Publication Data
Names: Futterknecht, John, author. | Seldman, Marty, author.
Title: Leading in the global matrix : proven skills & strategies to succeed
   in a collaborative world / by John Futterknecht and Marty Seldman.
Description: Dallas, TX : BenBella Books, [2020] | Includes index. |
Identifiers: LCCN 2019036330 | ISBN 9781948836494 (hardback) | ISBN
   9781948836746 (ebook)
Subjects: LCSH: Leadership. | Organizational change. | Organizational
   behavior.
Classification: LCC HD57.7 .F8649 2020 | DDC 658.4/092--dc23
LC record available at https://lccn.loc.gov/2019036330

Editing by Susan Lauzau
Copyediting by Scott Calamar
Proofreading by Greg Teague and Jenny Bridges
Indexing by WordCo Indexing Services
Text design by Publishers' Design and Production Services, Inc.
Text composition by PerfecType, Nashville, TN
Cover design by Kara Klontz
Cover image © Shutterstock/hunthomas
Printed by Lake Book Manufacturing

Distributed to the trade by Two Rivers Distribution, an Ingram brand
www.tworiversdistribution.com

Special discounts for bulk sales are available.
Please contact bulkorders@benbellabooks.com.

*To my wife, Luba, and daughter, Ariella.*
—John Futterknecht

*To my grandkids, Molly, Esther, Yonah, and Eliyahu.*
—Marty Seldman

*"Organization structures do not fail, but management fails at implementing them successfully."*

—Jay Galbraith, *Designing Matrix Organizations That Actually Work*

*"The challenge is not so much to build a matrix structure as it is to create a matrix in the minds of our managers."*

—Christopher A. Bartlett and Sumantra Ghoshal, "Matrix Management: Not a Structure, a Frame of Mind," *Harvard Business Review*

# Contents

❖

❖

# Working in a Matrixed World

## *Welcome to Business in the Twenty-First Century*

I N THE PAST DECADE, many global enterprises have transitioned from the traditional corporate hierarchy—where silo functions such as finance, HR, or operations and decentralized business units work with a high level of autonomy and independence—to a matrix model of cross-functional teams that work across a number of business units. The list of companies that have gravitated to this new, flatter type of organization includes IBM, Dow, Boeing, Starbucks, General Mills, Microsoft, and Citibank, among others. This shift is essentially a move away from a top-down, vertical leadership structure toward a more horizontal, integrated, and collaborative way of working.

The particular organizational design of the matrix structure varies from company to company: some institute formal structures organized around global centers of excellence (COEs), while other companies adopt highly fluid organizational designs with diffuse leadership and support, encompassing many parts of the business. Matrix structures can also evolve and transform over time as a result of leadership changes, shifts in strategy, and growth in organizational learning. Regardless of the precise structure or its stage of evolution, the matrix has become the dominant model for the global companies that are succeeding today. Among the compelling benefits prompting so many global companies to transition toward matrixed structures are:

- efficiencies and cost savings
- strategic thinking and innovation
- diversity of thought
- informed decision-making
- increased agility
- aligned execution
- improved organizational learning

However, for many organizations that have made the leap, the matrix hasn't fully delivered on its promise. Despite dedicating vast resources to preparing leaders for their new matrix roles, organizations struggle to harness the profound collaborative spirit that will generate the increased innovation and creative problem-solving the company seeks. As long-time executive coaches and leadership development experts who have more than six decades' combined experience, we know why.

Over the past several years, we've witnessed a clear trend in the focus of our coaching engagements. We are now routinely called on to help leaders develop and refine the skills they need to thrive in a matrix structure. Our assignments commonly begin with observations like these:

"We have a leader who is extremely talented, knows the business cold, and, historically, got great results for us . . . but so far she has struggled to get the same kind of traction in our new, more matrixed structure."

"We have a leader who has recently inherited a team that is working in a far more integrated fashion with multiple stakeholder groups, and he is having some challenges collaborating in the way we had hoped."

"We have a high-potential leader who has a strong track record of business success, strategic acumen, and great executive presence, but there are some questions around her ability to successfully influence without authority across our new matrix structure. We feel she needs to demonstrate these skills before we are confident about putting her into a more senior role."

What began as a few dozen of these matrix leadership–focused assignments became hundreds, allowing us to observe consistent sets of leadership challenges that cut across functions, business units, industries, and even continents. As we discovered, the challenges were not unique to one type of industry, role, geography, or organizational culture, but represented a constant, resulting from the move toward the matrix's greater complexity and its reliance on influence and collaboration rather than authority. Some core dynamics in the way individuals were now being asked to lead differed dramatically from their previous experience in more hierarchical structures. The shift from a more autonomous and independent way of leading to a more collaborative and interdependent style meant that the influence and alignment needed to drive decisions had increased exponentially. Leadership challenges in the matrix commonly manifest as:

- increased conflict and misunderstanding
- control issues and power struggles
- limited time and resources
- competing priorities and/or "turf" issues
- trust issues
- ambiguity around decision-making rights
- conflict between the pressure for delivering results with speed and the time needed to collaborate

When leaders do not develop the strategies and skills they need to overcome these obstacles, their ability to help their organizations achieve the benefits of a matrix structure is severely compromised.

The challenges, if unaddressed, predictably lead stakeholder groups who should be collaborating and leveraging each other's talent to get mired in conflict, undermining innovation and diversity of thought as the group members' trust breaks down. Frequently, these impediments mean that decision-making, projects, and initiatives grind to a halt. A VP of talent development described the impact of these leadership challenges in this way: "It's like we made a major investment to restructure our organization and provide all the necessary support to drive the business like a high-performing sports car designed to go one hundred miles per hour, but despite our efforts, we often find we are stuck driving at fifty miles per hour. And on some days, in reverse." This analogy captures perfectly our objective in writing this book: to provide leaders with the skills and strategies they need to drive their matrix organization to its full potential.

## COMPLEMENTING EXISTING ORGANIZATIONAL EFFORTS

Virtually all of our clients are aware of the increased complexities and challenges they face as they transition to the matrix. In fact, they tend to devote considerable resources to anticipating and meeting these challenges. We have seen organizations spend an extraordinary amount of time, financial resources, and attention in an effort to prime their leaders for success. These efforts include bringing in consulting companies to help develop a detailed structure, creating robust plans to communicate the purpose and benefits of the new structure internally, developing leadership behavior competency models, and providing internal collateral (i.e., brochures, presentations, videos, etc.) to explain how the business will transform from an operational standpoint.

All of these efforts are foundational and, based on our experience, no organization can introduce a successful matrix without them. However, even *with* these important support mechanisms, individual leaders and, by extension, organizations find that their matrix structure is not operating with the impact and efficiency they intended.

That is where *Leading in the Global Matrix* comes into play. While the above-mentioned efforts do a great job explaining *why* the organization is transitioning to a matrix and *what* is expected from its leaders, they miss a critical piece of the puzzle: *how* leaders must adapt to succeed in this new business environment. While leaders may understand the outlines of the new competencies, they may not know how to gain the skills necessary to demonstrate them. This book will teach you *how* to lead in a matrix.

## WHAT IS MISSING IN CURRENT MATRIX LEADERSHIP TRAINING

Based on our experience, organizational training programs focused on matrix leadership typically have two opportunities: bridge the gap between theory and practice, and navigate the unspoken dimensions of the matrix. We'll talk here about these challenges and how our approach complements the development strategies of our clients to address them.

### Bridging the Gap Between Theory and Practice

We have often been impressed by the depth of thought that organizations put into developing leadership competency models designed to help their executives succeed in their new matrixed organizations. Some of the commonly identified leadership abilities include:

- **Collaborating across boundaries**—Overcomes geographic and functional boundaries to drive key business objectives
- **Influencing without authority**—Effectively makes the case for change while anticipating multiple priorities and resistance, successfully bringing others along
- **Thinking strategically**—Brings an enterprise-wide perspective to discussions and generates innovative ideas to drive new business solutions

- **Building a broad network**—Continuously builds and maintains strategic relationships to strengthen collaboration and drive key initiatives
- **Demonstrating and encouraging a healthy exchange of ideas**—Displays the courage to surface difficult issues while demonstrating an open mind when challenged
- **Leading with inspiration**—Develops a vision that inspires others to follow and empowers others to achieve their full potential

These are just a few examples of competency expectations our clients have designed for their leaders. In some cases, the models are even more robust, rich, and sophisticated than this example, and they include a detailed breakdown of each identified skill area together with an explanation of how the skill is exemplified at various leadership levels (i.e., manager, director, VP, C-suite, etc.). Once the model has been developed, organizations communicate these plans throughout the company to establish clarity about the new behaviors of the future.

However, while most leaders intellectually grasp the behaviors associated with each of these competencies, when we ask them in confidential discussions, "Do you know *how* to execute these behaviors in real time, in the trenches of your complex day-to-day activities?", they often acknowledge that they don't. This is where the gap exists: leaders understand what is being asked of them, they just don't know how to execute it.

The natural question is, why? We see two main reasons.

1. Leaders have mental habits that stand in their way. Many people have powerfully ingrained habits that prevent them from adopting these new behaviors. Without an understanding of their limiting habits, leaders can't shift to the mindset they need to demonstrate the new behaviors consistently.
2. They underestimate the difficulty of mastering the new competencies. The new behaviors required of leaders in the matrix are advanced and laced with nuance, but they sound familiar. Even seasoned leaders can underestimate the finesse required to

do them well. They think, "I have been collaborating with and influencing stakeholders my entire career, this is a strength of mine." This conviction leads them to underestimate the complexity of the new skill; while some of the language is similar, the game has changed from checkers to three-dimensional chess.

## Navigating the Unspoken Dimensions of the Matrix

In addition to lacking the right mental habits and underestimating the complexity of necessary leadership skills, two other areas have considerable impact on the success of a leader working in a matrixed organization. These topics are inherently uncomfortable to discuss, complicated to address, and rarely tackled directly: human nature and organizational complexity. The very nature of a matrix guarantees that there will be times when individual leaders will feel conflicted about supporting decisions that appear, at least in the short term, to put them at a considerable disadvantage. Likewise, in a matrix structure, more stakeholders are engaged and less clarity around decision-making authority exists, yet power dynamics still exist in some form.

Because of the discomfort with discussing these topics, most leadership training programs either minimize them or leave them out completely. That means that some of the most important insights and understanding, and the resulting skills and strategies, are omitted.

Our approach is different. We think of ourselves as "inspirational pragmatists." We believe in human potential and each person's capacity for greatness. We believe in the opportunities the matrix offers because it is designed around the best attributes of human nature: collaboration, respect, curiosity, collective action, inclusion, and relationship building. We've seen what a matrix structure can achieve. When it works the way it's designed to, it delivers on enhanced agility, more innovation, greater cost savings, increased collaboration, and all its other promises. Furthermore, we are advocates of amplifying and reinforcing all of these positive attributes in individual human beings and in the collective as it supports a successful matrix structure. At the same time, we understand all too well the realities of human nature and organizational dynamics—and the negative impact these forces can have on matrix success if they are not engaged directly and skillfully. We do not view these domains as toxic or negative (unless they manifest themselves in extreme behaviors), but rather as a part of organizational reality that must be considered and mastered for a successful, comprehensive approach.

Our inspirational pragmatist approach is about acknowledging both the potential of the matrix and its practical aspects—and finding a way to blend them together, allowing values-based, high-integrity leaders to navigate the holistic reality of a matrix successfully. Then, and only then, can the organization fully experience the magic of the matrix.

## USE THIS BOOK TO ACCELERATE YOUR LEADERSHIP DEVELOPMENT

Understand that there is no silver bullet that will make leading in a matrix simple and eliminate the inherent complexities. However, we promise that if you consistently apply the skills we teach, your EQ—effectiveness quotient—will increase significantly. And these improvements, over the course of time, can have an extraordinary impact on the success of your organization and, ultimately, your own career.

Knowing what you lack is half the battle. Once you are aware of your major skill gaps and have a plan for closing them, you can experience resounding success. We've seen teams journey from states of near dysfunction to models of matrix efficiency. We've watched as best practices have been shared throughout a company's global operations. We've seen diversity of thought coupled with improved communication lead to disruptive innovation. And we've been gratified to see that when leaders embrace this unique mix of skills, the result is individual success. We've watched people go from being actively disengaged with their companies to finding meaning in their work, fostering new relationships within and between teams, and taking on leadership roles as a result of their personal and professional growth.

Think of developing the skills needed to lead in the matrix as a marathon, not a sprint. You have spent an enormous amount of time and energy running the first twenty-five miles but are now hitting a wall. This book is the tool that will help you run that last mile and get you across the finish line. We expect that you come to the table with a solid skill set, and that your organization has already implemented the right structures and models for the matrix. We are here to help you take your game to the next level, where your organizational impact and career trajectory can reach their full potential.

*Leading in the Global Matrix* covers ten key skill areas, with each chapter focusing on the nuances of a particular skill set. Throughout the book you will read case studies, all based on true stories (although disguised to maintain anonymity), designed to capture the types of scenarios we have witnessed dozens, if not hundreds, of times. If you find yourself thinking, "Hey, I experienced a version of that scenario earlier this year!" you'll understand just how common these patterns are.

Each of the chapters introduces proven, easy-to-learn strategies that you can apply immediately. To help you reinforce the learning and refresh yourself on concepts at a glance, each chapter includes a "Your Matrix Moment" feature that encapsulates the main points and serves as a helpful checklist as you work to enhance your leadership skills. Our goal is to create a highly practical learning journey for you as you build your matrix leadership action plan.

Filled with our field-tested advice for building collaborative relationships, growing your influence, and enhancing your communication and executive presence, *Leading in the Global Matrix* helps you and your teams unlock your full potential, allowing the matrix to deliver fully on its powerful promise.

# CHAPTER 1

❖

# Cultivating a Matrix
# Mindset

To help you develop the most effective strategies and comprehensive action plan for leading in the global matrix, we'll leverage
the latest research in cognitive psychology and neuropsychology, as well
as the powerful research on fixed and growth mindsets by psychologist Carol Dweck. Understanding how your own assumptions influence
your choices and behavior is key to developing the flexible and constructive mindset you need to succeed in matrix leadership.

There is a good chance that, during a leadership program or in your
own reading, you have come across the concept of *self-talk*, generally
described as the inner monologue continuously unfolding in our heads.
The concept of self-talk has its origins in cognitive psychology, the study
of our mental processes and how they affect our emotions and behavior.
This field of psychology has an extraordinary range of valuable applications, including numerous therapeutic ones, as well as in business,
sports, and performance training.

We promise not to dive too deeply into the workings of cognitive psychology; however, it is important to understand the connection between
our self-talk and the optimal matrix mindset. First, our mindset as it
relates to any topic, including the organizational matrix, is, essentially, a
combination of self-talk phrases that emerge and become habit when we
are presented with certain experiences or topics. If someone asked you
about your thoughts on matters such politics or parenting, for example,

some well-established beliefs would likely be triggered in your brain—these comprise your mindset in relationship to the particular topic.

Our self-talk is so powerful in influencing our behavior because of a fundamental cognitive psychology axiom: What we say to ourselves determines our emotions, and these, in turn, dictate our behavior. Furthermore, much of our self-talk is deeply ingrained and habitual, so certain events instantly trigger certain internal reactions. However, our self-talk (and, by default, our mindset) is also subconscious in nature; unless we take the time to reflect on it, the mental reaction occurs without intention. As the expression goes, "We rarely think about what we think about." This is a critical idea to appreciate because the matrix is likely to present you with circumstances that trigger self-talk that is less than helpful, and if you are not aware of it and able to refocus your thoughts, this harmful self-talk can lead to behavior that ranges from ineffective to downright damaging.

But there is good news. Whatever our current mindset toward the matrix, it does not need to remain fixed. In fact, one of the most encouraging and empowering discoveries in neuropsychology is the concept of neuroplasticity—that our brains, including our thoughts and mindset, are entirely capable of changing in response to new information. Therefore, if we can become aware of our current mindsets in relationship to the matrix, we can choose practices that allow us to move beyond our limiting beliefs.

One of the most prominent researchers in the area of mindset, Dr. Carol Dweck, has written extensively on the topic (including *Mindset: The New Psychology of Success*) and how it permeates nearly every aspect of our lives. Our mindsets limit our potential or power our success; mindset can mark the difference between mediocrity and excellence. Mindset influences our self-awareness, our self-esteem, our creativity, our resilience, our level of depression, and our tendency to stereotype, among other things. Dweck's research focuses on a powerful yet simple belief: there are fixed mindsets and growth mindsets, representing the opposite ends of a spectrum.

People with a fixed mindset believe that talents and abilities are innate—who you are is who you are, period. To this way of thinking, characteristics such as intelligence and creativity are fixed, rather than traits that can be developed. Those with a growth mindset believe that abilities can be cultivated through effort. Yes, people differ greatly—in their aptitude, interests, or temperaments—but everyone can change and grow through application and experience.

Dweck explains that it's entirely possible to have a mindset that is not wholly growth or fixed, and to lean a certain way in one area of life but a different way in other areas. Your set of assumptions may thus be different when it comes to artistic talent, intelligence, personality, or creativity. Whatever mindset you have in a particular area will guide your behavior in that area.

How does the concept of fixed versus growth mindset change behavior? A fixed mindset creates the sense that you are simply limited in certain areas, as well as spurring an urgency to prove yourself. Criticism is seen as an attack on your character, something to be avoided. A growth mindset, on the other hand, encourages effort and practice. Criticism is seen as valuable feedback and openly embraced. The hallmark of a growth mindset is dedication to sticking with a task or project, especially when things are not going well. Not surprisingly, those with a growth mindset are more likely to thrive, as they believe they have the capacity to gain proficiency and master new challenges; they are not limited to the talents they were "born with."

So, let's get to work cultivating a mindset that will help you grow as a leader. In this chapter, you will learn how to raise your self-awareness around the most critical matrix mindset success factors and discover self-talk phrases that will help you cultivate a more optimal mindset.

## "THEORY" MINDSET VERSUS "DAY TO DAY" MINDSET

Don't underestimate the importance of mindset in priming yourself for success in matrix leadership. Without the right mindset, you won't be appropriately disposed to execute the behaviors and strategies you need to get the most out of yourself and your team. As you read about mindset, you may be saying to yourself, "Actually, I am not worried about this area. I have been on board with the new matrix structure from day one, and I believe in the potential of the matrix." We are sure that is true, and perhaps you have mastered the optimal matrix mindset.

However, like many who have started a diet and felt passionately about losing weight, defeating self-talk may rise up in challenging moments. During these times of high stress, your diet self-talk may be, "I will feel better if I eat this junk food," and, when the weekend approaches, the self-talk that creeps in is, "I worked hard this week and I deserve this delicious cake." Your principled agreement with the diet doesn't stand up when you try to put it into practice.

In the same way, your initial self-talk regarding the matrix structure can easily fall apart when difficulties begin. Your internal monologue may start off sounding like this: "I know that working in a matrixed fashion is what is best for our business over the long term. I am committed and up for the challenge." Then you find yourself under the gun to deliver a project; your supervisor has sent you two emails saying that she is counting on you to deliver results by the end of the week. However, you know that, in order to drive the project forward in a collaborative, matrixed fashion, you will need to engage and persuade several important stakeholders who are not entirely in agreement with your approach. In this moment, your self-talk could easily shift to: "Ideally, I should drive this project forward collaboratively to gain others' input and establish alignment, but that might take considerable time and energy and push back my ability to make the decision. In this case, I am just going to make a decision on my own without consulting them. Next time, when I am not feeling so much deadline pressure, I'll make sure the process is more inclusive."

What we are after when we talk about developing the matrix mindset is a mindset that is not only in theoretical agreement (that's the easy part) but is prepared with awareness and resilience, and shows up when we need it most—in the trenches, during times of stress, complexity, and difficulty. When you have developed this capacity, during scenarios like the one outlined above, you will have the clarity and focus to tell yourself, "Although it may seem more convenient in the short term to leave out the additional stakeholders, I know that over the long term it is likely to negatively impact trust. That can lead to a breakdown of communication and collaboration and cost us much more time and productivity down the road. I'm going to take the right course of action now and ensure that all the relevant stakeholders feel included." The ability to consistently focus on the correct, long-term collaborative behaviors is vital to matrix leadership.

## MATRIX MINDSET SUCCESS FACTORS

The matrix mindset success factors are the top four areas that impact leaders in the matrix, in either a positive or negative manner. Unless you address these four factors and foster a mindset prepared to contend with them in a practical way, you will struggle to find your highest success in the matrix. These four areas are:

1. Overcoming loss of autonomy
2. Dealing with anxiety, uncertainty, and loss of confidence
3. Demonstrating empathy
4. Cultivating curiosity

As you read about each of the matrix mindset factors, we encourage you to reflect on which of these areas are most valuable for you. To be clear, none of your current mental tendencies is "wrong," but pause to consider whether certain mindset habits are influencing you in a way that inhibits your success. If some of your mental habits are holding you back, you could benefit from developing greater self-awareness and intentionally cultivating a mindset that helps you move beyond any current limiting beliefs.

Please remember that, to a certain degree, we are all inclined to give ourselves positive reviews; we give ourselves the benefit of the doubt, assuming that we bring an ideal mindset to each circumstance. Be as objective as possible in analyzing your own attitudes and behavior. If you find yourself wondering how you perform in one of the areas, check in with a colleague you trust and ask how you actually show up in those particular circumstances. For instance, you might say to a trusted colleague: "It is my intention to engage in our matrix meetings in a way that balances offering my perspective with demonstrating curiosity, agility, and an open mind to others' perspectives, so we can arrive at the best possible answers. That said, I know that my intentions will not always match my impact, and I am sure I have blind spots. As you have observed me in a number of these meetings, what could I do differently that would help me achieve that goal?" You may be fortunate enough to receive some invaluable feedback related to your body language, your listening tendencies, or your choice of words that you can adjust to make your meeting presence more effective.

## Overcoming Loss of Autonomy

One area of frustration concerns a loss of autonomy and control, and the feeling that things are more complex, difficult, and take longer in the new matrix structure, though the pressure to drive results with speed has only increased. Although any leader could develop this particular frustration in relationship to the matrix, we have found it to be most widespread among those who identify themselves as type A personalities. Often, these leaders are inherently more comfortable in circumstances where they feel they have independence and clarity with regard to resources and decision-making, which tend to decrease in the matrix. If you have ever been referred to as a control freak, the loss of autonomy associated with working in the matrix is likely to push your buttons.

### Negative Self-Talk

Listen for internal conversations that include a lot of negative patter. Some common mindset patterns and negative self-talk include:

- "The lack of clarity and true ownership creates so much confusion and delay."
- "It seems like we spend so much time aligning stakeholders that nothing actually gets done."
- "The matrix has us so internally focused that we are not prioritizing our competition and big bets."

- "Somehow, I am supposed to be accountable for results, but I don't have the decision-making independence or resources to execute in the way I think is best. How is that fair?"

### Outcomes of Negative Self-Talk

Recall the mindset formula: Our beliefs determine our emotions, which dictate our behaviors. Given that reality, negative self-talk can lead to maladaptive behavior such as:

- a tendency to withhold information from some stakeholders—this can lead not only to trust issues but also to incomplete decision-making
- communication (verbal or written), brought on by frustration, that is considered abrasive and creates conflict
- disengaging from certain initiatives because of a feeling that ownership is unclear and it is not worth getting overly involved

### Ask Yourself

Think back to times when you may have had negative thoughts and ask yourself:

- "Did this mindset help me or did it hurt me?"
- "Was I stewing or was I doing?" That is, am I wallowing in my frustration or am I taking positive action to solve the problem?
- "What impact did my frustration/anger have?"

### Helpful Self-Talk

Next time you are in a situation where you feel frustrated or angry, try using one of these helpful self-talk scripts:

- "It is sometimes true that collaborating with stakeholders in a matrix takes more time, but the benefits when we achieve our goal are critical to the success of the business."

- "Go slow to go fast: By investing time and energy, we can build strong, trusted stakeholder partnerships that will allow us to work much more efficiently and effectively going forward. It is worth the investment!"
- "All I can control is my own behavior, so that is what I will focus on. Getting frustrated about what is out of my control is not going to help me or the organization succeed."
- "Am I stewing or am I doing? Am I stuck simply 'stewing' about my frustration, which will only make matters worse? Or is my frustration serving a catalyst that gets me to go *do* something—to take constructive action—to solve the issue. The power of this question is that it holds up a mirror and shows us that getting stuck in our frustration is not helping us or the organization—it is a reminder to get un-stuck and focus on fruitful action."

## Dealing with Anxiety, Uncertainty, and Loss of Confidence

Anxiety, uncertainty, and a loss of confidence are other emotional reactions that can form an undercurrent when an organization shifts toward the matrix. These emotions are completely understandable, and they typically result from a fear of the rate of change, questions about what the new approach means for your career, and doubts about whether you possess the skills you need to be successful in this new environment. With all the shifts in organizational structure, you may wonder whether your role will even exist in the future.

### Negative Self-Talk

Mindset patterns and self-talk surrounding anxiety and uncertainty sound like this:

- "It seems that, if you haven't worked at a consulting firm in your prior life, you can't be successful in the new environment."
- "There is so much change, who knows what is actually here to stay? Sometimes it seems that if we just wait it out, we will go back to the way we used to work."

- "I had a clear career path before this change occurred, but now I don't know where I stand with the organization and what my path forward is."

## Outcomes of Negative Self-Talk

This kind of negativity, if it persists, can lead to a variety of suboptimal behavior:

- a tendency to "passively" resist the implementation of the new global strategies out of fear that they may be personally disadvantageous
- subpar performance and poor leadership brought on by a lack of confidence
- a mentality that favors a wait-and-see approach rather than asking the important questions and leaning in to the challenges

## Ask Yourself

Think back to times when you may have had these negative thoughts, and ask yourself:

- "Was my fear a possibility or a probability?"
- "If the scenario I am worried about actually happens, would it constitute an inconvenience or a catastrophe?"
- "Am I stuck in worrying, or am I focused on planning to minimize the risk I am concerned about?"

## Helpful Self-Talk

Next time you are in a situation where you are feeling anxious, uncertain, or underconfident, bolster yourself with the following self-talk statements:

- "The best players stay on the field. If I focus on performing at the highest level of which I am capable, I will give myself the best chance for success, regardless of how much change takes place."

- "Embracing change and demonstrating the agility to pivot as the organization needs is not only key to the success of the business, it will reflect positively on me and my career potential."
- "I know that I have the ability to learn and grow as a leader. It is true that this new environment will require me to evolve some of my skills, but with time and focus I am confident I can get there."

## Demonstrating Empathy

Empathy, our next matrix area, may be a subtle quality, but it is a potential game changer for leaders who keep it top of mind and demonstrate it regularly. By design, the highly integrated structure of the matrix creates scenarios in which many more stakeholders are part of decision-making and execution; to complicate matters, these stakeholders are from very different parts of the organization and have different perspectives and priorities. This makes moments of empathy critical.

### Negative Self-Talk

Negative mindset patterns and self-talk in the area of empathy include:

- "Obviously, nobody understands the true needs of my local market better than I do; how can the center of excellence believe they have the best ideas when they are so far removed?"
- "We are the center of excellence for a reason. Why don't they listen and implement what we are telling them?"
- "Bob is just not pulling his weight on this project. He always seems to be the bottleneck because we are dependent on him and his team to deliver. Where is the sense of urgency?"
- "Why is Jennifer weighing in on this decision when she is not even from my function? She doesn't understand the situation like I do and is pulling us in the wrong direction."
- "Why is Eduardo so resistant? We have clearly laid out why our strategy is the right one, and yet he just won't get fully on board. I feel like he has his own agenda."

*Outcomes of Negative Self-Talk*

If you have ever found yourself having these types of thoughts and emotions, we can assure you that you are not alone. Every one of these thoughts is entirely understandable given the complexity of the matrix. However, there is a real risk that these frustrations will fester and build momentum; if that happens, they can snowball into debilitating matrix behaviors. Below are some of the common negative results:

- a belief that you are in an us versus them situation
- lack of trust
- an unwillingness to share information and provide feedback
- close-mindedness and failure to look for the win-win

What is the antidote to falling into this negative mindset trap? One word: empathy. We have coached countless teams and individual stakeholders trying to "collaborate" and facing these kinds of feelings. Individually and collectively, they fall deeper and deeper into this rabbit hole of emotions, where one negative belief leads to another; that cycle leads people to jump to conclusions and attribute negative motives to others, which then leads to protective, competitive, and non-collaborative behaviors. At this point, the classic self-fulling prophecy ensues. As lack of trust and concern for self-preservation lead to the behaviors above, discussion is likely to become guarded and more aggressive, which only validates the negative beliefs.

However, we have also had the opportunity to work with leaders who did not get caught up in these destructive cycles and managed to maintain a positive perspective about their stakeholders, even when circumstances became challenging. When we asked them to share their secret, their responses were very consistent:

- "We are all in the same boat."
- "I remind myself that their role and circumstance is as dynamic and complex as mine."

Perhaps you are one of those individuals who can maintain a constructive mindset and high level of empathy under stress and pressure. Congratulations! If, on the other hand, you identify with the frustrations and negative cycles described earlier, you can work to develop your sense of empathy in those difficult moments.

### Ask Yourself

Maintaining empathy in difficult moments requires that you shift your focus from the frustration you are experiencing to the viewpoint of the other person(s)—you must put yourself in the other person's shoes:

- "I wonder what kind of pressure this stakeholder is under based on the objectives she has been given by her boss?"
- "As I look at the big picture, I'm curious whether this stakeholder may have lost some autonomy and could be feeling frustrated or insecure?"
- "Are there any implications to this stakeholder's career path that I should be sensitive to if we move ahead in this direction?"

### Helpful Self-Talk

Make a habit of reminding yourself to consider the experiences of other team members. Your understanding can go a long way toward fostering the positive, trusting relationship among your matrix stakeholders that is essential for successful collaboration:

- "We are in this together. There is a good chance we are all feeling some of these similar frustrations from time to time."
- "By being intentional in offering my empathy, it will help me build trust and give me important insights into how to best collaborate with this stakeholder."

## Cultivating Curiosity

Saying that leaders ought to encourage their own curiosity might seem akin to saying, "It is important to listen." And yet, in a matrix, a disposition toward curiosity is essential for a multitude of reasons. First, the purpose of the matrix is to engender diversity of thought—leveraging insights, experience, and wisdom from a broad range of perspectives so the team can arrive at the best possible decision. Second, in a matrix environment, you are often required to influence without authority and bring stakeholders along through persuasion. In order to achieve this, you need to listen authentically and have genuine interest in the perspectives and ideas of others.

Your stakeholders are likely to shut down if you give them the impression that you believe you have all the answers, your mind is made up, and you are at this meeting primarily to educate them. While curiosity is obviously a good thing and, as a result, the idea that leaders demonstrate it consistently might be logical, the facts fly in the face of many leaders' long-established mental habits. Many acknowledge freely that they are competitive by nature (competition is a trait we generally believe has tremendous upside) and think of meetings as their opportunity to shine, demonstrate their thought leadership, and drive the agenda forward. To be clear, a strong presence at meetings and excellent communication and influencing skills are essential (so much so that we devote an entire chapter to this later in the book), but you also need to be open to others' contributions and show that you are willing to partner with others to solve challenges.

### Negative Self-Talk

When you go into meetings, refrain from the following types of self-talk:

- "This is my one chance to stand out and get these stakeholders on board, so I need to drive the conversation."

- "With so many competing priorities, I need to be aggressive and push our agenda forward; otherwise, it won't get the attention we need."
- "Meetings are my most important opportunity to demonstrate my expertise and thought leadership. I need to fight for airtime and take full advantage."

*Outcomes of Negative Self-Talk*

If you display a lack of genuine curiosity, your behavior, even if subtle, can hamper collaboration dramatically. The effects of such behavior include:

- stakeholders' perception that you care only about your own agenda
- discussions that fail to be truly inclusive
- suppression of valuable perspective and ideas
- poor stakeholder relationships

*Ask Yourself*

Think back to times when you may have attended a meeting with the mindset that your chosen approach was the best course, and ask yourself:

- "How did others perceive my actions?"
- "Were the results of my approach positive or negative?"
- "Did I create an environment of true collaboration?"

*Helpful Self-Talk*

When attending a meeting, show up not only with great ideas for your own plan but also with authentic curiosity and an open mind toward other people's ideas. Here are a few self-talk questions that will help:

- "What experience do these individuals have that I don't?"
- "What perspective and information have they been exposed to that I haven't?"

- "What are they better at than I am?"
- "There is no way for one person to have all the answers and information. How can I learn from others in this meeting?"

Although these are very simple questions, focusing on them automatically turns your attention to the benefits of listening and learning.

## STRATEGIES FOR IMPLEMENTING YOUR MINDSET PRACTICE

The good news is that cultivating a strong matrix mindset is extremely achievable and will position you for success. The challenge is that an understanding of the necessary mindset is almost worthless if you do not know how to put it into practice. Positive self-talk only works if you do it, and do it consistently. Remember, you are working against powerfully ingrained habits that are not going to go away based on "aha" moments alone. The key is to develop your personal plan and then execute it.

Below are four ways to cultivate a matrix mindset—you may choose more than one.

1. **Start your day with a "check-up from the neck up."** You can do this on your commute to work. Spend just two or three minutes reflecting and practicing your helpful self-talk, and you will begin your day with the right mindset.

2. **Prepare for key matrix meetings.** In addition to preparing your content and communication strategies, ensure that your mindset is in the optimal place before key meetings. Give yourself two or three minutes before a meeting starts to reflect on your helpful self-talk phrases. This is time extremely well spent.

3. **Place reminders near your computer and in other visible spots.** So much of your matrix communication happens via email, conference call, and other communication technologies. Place

helpful self-talk phrases next to each of these devices to serve as quick reminders before you draft that email or join that call. These notes can also come in handy as in-the-moment meditations if an email or conversation point pushes one of your buttons.

---

### YOUR MATRIX MOMENT: CULTIVATING A MATRIX MINDSET

- Consider the mindset formula: Our beliefs determine our emotions, which dictate our behaviors.
- Remember the four matrix mindset success factors:

  1. Overcoming loss of autonomy
  2. Dealing with anxiety, uncertainty, and loss of confidence
  3. Demonstrating empathy
  4. Cultivating curiosity

- Watch out for negative self-talk that can derail you as you work to cultivate the matrix mindset success factors. If you catch yourself engaged in negative self-talk, get back on track by asking yourself questions like:

  - "Does this mindset help me or does it hurt me?"
  - "Am I focused on what I can control to help achieve the best outcome in this situation?"
  - "How do others perceive my actions?"
  - "Are the results of my approach positive or negative?"
  - "If the scenario I am worried about actually happens, would it constitute an inconvenience or a catastrophe?"
  - (See additional helpful questions throughout the chapter.)

- Our self-talk is habitual–strengthen your matrix mindset by establishing internal monologues that are positive, productive, and motivating.

---

4. **Ensure that your team cultivates a matrix mindset.** If you have direct reports, your matrix mindset is arguably even more essential because your disposition and behavior will have tremendous influence on the mindset of the entire team. Make no mistake, if you get off a conference call and vent your frustrations to your team about the challenges of the matrix structure or difficult stakeholders, you will shape their perspective. The best practice is to intentionally cultivate the matrix mindset with your entire team. We encourage you to discuss the importance of mindset openly with your team and ask each of them to develop his or her own action plan. From time to time, spend a portion of a meeting asking the team how they are feeling and what their current mindset is.

## CREATING YOUR MATRIX
## MINDSET ACTION PLAN

As we've mentioned, the best way to build the right matrix mindset is by having a plan and practicing the skills associated with a positive mindset on a regular basis. Here is your opportunity to start building your own mindset action plan with some self-reflection exercises.

- Think back to the four matrix mindset success factors. Which resonates most for you? Why?
- How often do you find yourself "stuck" in negative emotions (i.e., hourly, daily, weekly, etc.)?
- How are your work and productivity affected when you find yourself trapped in these negative scenarios?
- Which of the self-talk skills in this chapter did you find most helpful and which do you plan to use?
- Use the chart to create your personal mindset action plan.

## Mindset Action Plan

| Negative Mindset Scenarios | Self-Talk I Plan to Use | Implementation Strategy |
|---|---|---|
|  |  |  |
|  |  |  |
|  |  |  |

## A FINAL WORD ON MINDSET

Successful leadership in the matrix is rooted in your mindset. Cultivating supportive self-talk and the resulting attitudes and behavior are key to developing and sharpening a breadth of matrix leadership skills. That's why it is so important that you set aside time to regularly reflect on your mindset and focus your thoughts in ways that build and maintain it—and which minimize the unhelpful inner dialogue that will derail you.

The good news is that your mindset can be improved with practice—if yours is not in an ideal place, work to change it. You now have the tools you need to foster a mindset that will set you on a path to matrix success.

CHAPTER 2

❖

# Building and Maintaining Trust

T RUST IS ONE OF the most important elements of matrix success. It is also the most fragile. Most of us are familiar with the concept known as the speed of trust—this is the rate at which change can occur, based not on concrete factors such as resources but on the human bonds that support us as we take risks and venture into the unknown. In the matrix world, sustainable change happens not on any external timeline but at the speed of trust. It stands to reason, then, that the most important enabler of swift progress and nimble collaboration is a strong culture of trust.

It is equally true that, when trust breaks down, collaboration and speed suffer and change may come to a grinding halt. The challenge of working in complex matrix structures can lead even high-integrity individuals to inadvertently commit "trust busters"—acts that undermine or even dismantle trusting relationships.

In this chapter, we'll look closely at the role of trust in the matrix, and we'll examine the ways a leader's actions can build or bust that vital emotional bond. Most important, we'll detail practical ways to build trust, along with equally critical ways to avoid damaging it. Embracing trust practices and avoiding trust busters are both crucial—these two strategies work in concert to create the climate necessary for matrix success.

# MATRIX TRUST: MORE THAN
# GOOD INTENTIONS

As we begin, let's define our terms. We all get gut feelings that tell us who and what we trust, but how does that intuition play out in a workplace environment, specifically a matrix environment? While trust is crucial to all human progress, it is much more important in a matrix structure than in a traditional hierarchical structure because of a key underlying premise of the matrix: by working together in an interdependent, collaborative way, as the matrix demands, we can arrive at the best possible solutions for the organization in the long term.

That commitment to collaborative solutions and the organization's well-being asks for a lot of trust. It submits that as an individual stakeholder—or as part of a stakeholder group—for any initiative or project, you have the outlook that the solution evaluated as the best may not be ideal for you in the short term. It might not help you achieve your goals as immediately or as dramatically as another course would. In fact, it may feel as if the decision favors another stakeholder group. However, you respect and understand that the final decision is the best one from a broader organizational perspective.

This is doable if the underlying feeling stakeholders have about one another and about the organization is fundamentally one of trust. The attitude must be: "We're all in this together and we understand that, at any given moment, we may feel like we have to give up something or extend trust somewhere, but as a result of the collective success we will have, the rising tide will lift all ships." The belief in an ultimate positive outcome—that unspoken agreement—is a necessary quality. That defines a culture of trust.

On the other hand, if a question arises about whether such trust exists, if stakeholders ever say to themselves, "Hey, this isn't ideal for me, and I need to jockey for my best position so I can win in the end," everyone reverts to competing. The organization's dynamic is very different depending upon whether the people who work together trust one another.

We're not talking here about the split between high-integrity people and what we might call bad actors, individuals who willfully lie, fudge numbers, or steal from the company. That is a whole different topic. We're looking at how to build and maintain trust among individuals who are essentially trustworthy. We're starting with the assumption that those you're working with are high-integrity, well-intentioned people who want the organization to win. And yet, with all their good traits, high-integrity people in the matrix—because of its unique nature and complexity—may act in ways that impact and undermine trust.

We know this is a common issue because we hear it all the time. A series of questions we ask our audiences when we're delivering programs on trust in the matrix goes like this: "If we were to send out a survey across your particular organization and ask, 'Are you trustworthy?' what answer would you give?" Most of the time we get 100 percent of our audience members saying yes, they are trustworthy.

Next we ask, "What percentage of your organization do you believe would agree with you about that?" Most say 100 percent of the organization. Maybe there are a couple of honest sociopaths in the mix, but for the most part, an extremely high percentage answer that they are both trustworthy and trusted.

Then we ask the critical question: "Have you ever had an experience in this matrix environment where one of your colleagues or stakeholders has behaved in a way that has negatively impacted your level of trust in them?" Almost 100 percent of them respond yes.

So, we know we have a disconnect. How can organizations be full of high-integrity people and yet simultaneously have a high rate of people whose trust is being undermined? This tells us that even well-intentioned leaders in matrix environments often, albeit inadvertently, behave in ways that undercut their colleagues' trust. This is why good intentions and a strong value system are only the beginning. In our coaching and leadership development sessions, we have heard hundreds of examples of strong leaders who *intended* well with a particular action or behavior, yet their conduct landed wrong on the other party. The *impact* of that misstep was broken trust. Because of the inherent complexity of the matrix environment, leaders need to approach building and maintaining trust as a highly deliberate behavioral discipline. Intention alone is not enough.

Trust is not something you can assume to be present and functioning. It is fluid, usually either cycling in a positive direction or cycling in a detrimental direction. Because it is rarely static, trust in a matrix needs to be embraced as a daily discipline, something that is top of mind in virtually every interaction. Remember that there's a great deal riding on team members' mutual trust, and it is easily broken.

When we reviewed the story of a medical device company and its senior vice president of quality, we found a classic case of a leader with the best of intentions who breached the trust of stakeholders and started a damaging cycle of mistrust that was not easy to reverse.

## CASE STUDY: WHEN INTENT FAILS

When our client, a US-based medical device company, went looking for a senior vice president for quality, its search firm connected the company with Ernesto S., an engineer who had secured his PhD at New York's Cooper Union. Ernesto's passion for biology and chemistry, plus his background helping companies navigate the regulations of the FDA, made him an attractive candidate. He took the job and brought with him his training, his experience, and his core commitment to integrity and honesty.

Ernesto came to the new job with a strong sense of his own process. He was, he often said, willing to deliver a "tough love" message. He considered his chief responsibility to be communicating ways to improve processes and raise standards, even if this ruffled some feathers. "I am definitely not running a popularity contest," he said.

In his first months with the company, Ernesto took steps to change the quality reporting process, explaining to some plant managers that, in the future, they would report certain information directly to him. He was pleased to discover an old friend working at the company, an individual with whom he'd worked at a previous employer. That friend quickly became a close confidant.

The true test for Ernesto came when he made a site visit to a Mexican production plant. During the visit, Ernesto thought the on-site quality manager seemed anxious. He encouraged her to tell him her concerns, and he assured her he would keep her account confidential. So the manager shared her worries about quality issues at the plant, and Ernesto swung into action immediately. He confronted the plant manager before he left Mexico, and he sent an email to the head of manufacturing accusing him of "putting the resources and reputation of the company at risk."

That set off a series of events that took place mostly out of Ernesto's earshot. The Mexican quality manager, who had been promised confidentiality, told her peers that Ernesto was a "loose cannon" who did not keep promises and could put a plant at risk. The head of manufacturing, targeted in Ernesto's email, launched a campaign to persuade his fellow execs that Ernesto had been a poor pick for the job and was not a good culture fit. And finally, within Ernesto's own team, members began to say they did not trust Ernesto because he "played favorites" and kept closest counsel with his personal friend from a previous job.

Ernesto was unaware of most of this, although he began to notice an uptick in people either withholding information from him or being slow to provide him with data he needed.

The conflict came to a head at an off-site senior leadership meeting. Ernesto gave a presentation on quality problems and emphasized the need to raise the bar on best practices to ensure that their company maintained consumer trust. At that point, the head of manufacturing interrupted: "Trust. I don't think you should use that word. People in glass houses shouldn't throw stones."

Ernesto was surprised and visibly upset. He asked the head of manufacturing what he meant by that. And the head of manufacturing was more than happy to elaborate—and escalate. "What it means is that, since you have not even earned the trust of your team, you should be the last person to stand there and lecture us on trust!"

The meeting devolved: Ernesto accused the head of manufacturing of sloppy, dangerous practices. The head of manufacturing continued his attack on Ernesto's trustworthiness. The exchange got so heated that several people in the room thought the men might come to physical blows. The CEO had to step in and call for a break to diffuse the clash.

That's how quickly trust can unravel. In the course of just a few months, Ernesto went from champion of best practices to Public Enemy No. 1.

And the trust destruction process does not always require an event as obvious as Ernesto's failure to keep the Mexican director's confidence. It can be a smaller, quieter trigger, such as a team member on a conference call failing to really listen or appearing to undervalue or deprioritize other people's agendas. Any of these scenarios is enough for other stakeholders in the discussion to end that conference call or step out of the meeting with a negative feeling.

## UNDERSTANDING TRUST CYCLES

To avoid a crisis of trust, it's important to understand the nature of this emotional state. As we noted earlier, trust is never static. It is in a constant state of flux, influenced by the behavior of the interacting people. This is why the best way to create and cultivate trust is to actively manage trust cycles, both the vicious and the virtuous. Let's look at each.

### The Vicious Trust Cycle

A breakdown of trust can start with the most ordinary of events. Stakeholders get together to solve a problem or address an issue and something goes awry. Perhaps, as in the case study, a person breaks a confidence, or maybe another difficulty emerges, such as a lack of understanding about a certain decision.

Often, small breaches of trust and minor misunderstandings can be cleared up with a quick conversation. But that is not what usually happens. Most of the time, people get frustrated. They don't check in to find out the reasons for the other person's actions. Instead, they go to their colleagues, their friends, their inner circle, and start to bad-mouth: "Can you believe so-and-so did that? Wow. Clearly he is just not a team player. It's all about him and his priorities."

Predictably, emotions like frustration kick in. Because again, in this matrix environment, stakeholders can begin to think, "Hey, now I'm being set up to fail!" In some way, the situation becomes competitive. So what happens from there in the trust cycle? Not only do we have the original stakeholders who felt they were negatively impacted, we now also have the folks who heard all the bad-mouthing. They may start to talk among themselves and share that frustration or vent to others. And that may influence the way they communicate with other stakeholders.

In a negative cycle, good things go bad and bad things get worse. Now, the people caught in the cycle are not sharing as much information. They're not sharing as many ideas. They're not providing feedback. Then, subgroups start to form—us vs. them. There's even more resistance to ideas on the team. There's less collaboration. What you end up with is a whole lot of CYA ("cover your ass") behavior, and this cycle can continue to spiral downward.

It's essential to say here that vicious trust cycles are very common, and they are not indicative of a poorly functioning organization or bad people. When we work with leaders and we present the concept, most people will raise their hands and share that they're either currently observing such a cycle, are in a vicious trust cycle, or have experienced one within the past three to six months.

It is emotionally unpleasant and distracting to be caught in a vicious trust cycle—that alone is toxic and damaging—but this scenario also has serious business implications. Beyond simply creating an unfavorable working environment, these cycles can bring collaboration to a grinding halt. Decisions and processes can slow dramatically because the free flow of information isn't there—that speed of trust doesn't exist. Every matter becomes a political football that needs to be escalated to senior leadership, who then gets frustrated and asks, "Why can't you guys just collaborate?"

Vicious cycles are enormously damaging. A major premise of the matrix structure is that it creates collaboration, which leads to velocity and growth. In fact, vicious trust cycles can produce the opposite experience: the loss of trust slows things down, processes and decision-making are inefficient, and the organization fails to reap the benefits of the diversity, aligned execution, and shared best practices because there's division in the ranks.

## The Virtuous Trust Cycle

The good news is that, while a great deal of negativity can come out of a vicious trust cycle, a virtuous trust cycle can produce extraordinarily positive results. In a virtuous trust cycle, team members have faith in one another and their joint commitment to the organization, and a positive sense of collaboration prevails. If things do go sideways, or if somebody forgets to share something or is having an off day and is a little abrupt, there's a greater likelihood that others will assume positive intent.

In a virtuous trust cycle, a true sense of collaboration and partnership exists—teammates have the sense that "we're all in this together." Credit is shared, ideas surge, and more information flows. Because the people working together respect one another and are aligned with the organization's goals, they feel comfortable having a healthy debate—a critical aspect of the matrix structure. It is out of such spirited debates that innovations are sparked and strategic decisions are made. And, of course, people are much more likely to be open to feedback and learning when they hear from teammates they trust.

When you establish and maintain virtuous trust cycles, you reap the benefits that the matrix was designed to achieve. But it is not always easy to do. Throughout the remainder of this chapter, we'll focus on the insights, skills, and strategies that will help you cultivate a virtuous trust cycle, so your team members communicate more openly and share the best of their thinking.

## THE WORKING TRUST MODEL

We've developed a working trust model that gives you a defined way to understand the trust cycle, to be clear whether you have the kind of trust that will strengthen a situation or you are risking a vicious cycle. Our working trust model runs from zero to 10. Zero means you have no trust for a particular individual and would hardly turn your back for fear of what the person might do. Ten represents absolute trust. You would trust this individual with your money, your family, your children. Such a high level of trust is, of course, very rare. You'd be fortunate to have this ultimate level of trust with a handful of people in your life, much less with someone at work.

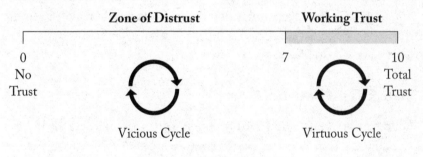

FIG. 2–1   **Working Trust**

We're focused on cultivating and maintaining trust somewhere between the levels of 7 and 10. This is what we call *working trust*. When you are situated within this range, you convey to stakeholders that you understand they're human beings with a healthy self-interest and their own career goals. But you simultaneously have no question that they genuinely care about the organization's success and also about yours. Each person in the interaction displays balanced self-interest. When that is the case, the team's positive, virtuous-cycle behavior is enabled.

## HOW TO BUILD AND MAINTAIN TRUST

We hope that we have convinced you that trust is not only essential to the success of a matrix structure, but also that it can easily be broken, even by high-integrity individuals who have the best intentions. As we move forward, we will take you beyond intention and show you how to "do" trust, specifically in the unique matrix environment. We will explain how you can give yourself, your team, and your organization the best opportunity to spend most of your time in virtuous trust cycles, reaping the benefits of the matrix while minimizing vicious cycles and their impact.

To encourage virtuous cycles, we must first examine the common behaviors that lead high-integrity leaders to inadvertently break trust. Then, we will move from analyzing the problem to solving it, outlining the day-to-day trust practices essential to fostering and preserving trust with your stakeholders.

### Matrix Trust Busters

Following are some of the most common matrix trust busters. By understanding the behaviors that break trust, we are better able to avoid these traps ourselves and to keep our teams out of vicious trust cycles.

#### Failure to Do What You Say You Will

Keeping your commitments and following through are critical in the matrix. Arguably, these traits are even more imperative than they are in hierarchical organizations because the level of interdependence is high in a matrix organization.

Many matrix projects rely on contributions from various stakeholder groups. If someone is not delivering his or her commitment in a timely fashion, the delay not only holds up an entire project (which is frustrating enough), it also makes executives and team members feel personally vulnerable because they are criticized by their respective leaders for the lack of progress. Explanations that they are not achieving the benchmark goals they expected because they are not getting what they need from other stakeholders may be perceived as excuses. This engenders frustration over the lack of speed, but it also begins to be personal: "Jeremy is making me look bad in front of my boss and clearly doesn't care. I guess I am just not important enough for him to prioritize his time."

However, leaders in the matrix are extremely busy in the "do more with less" environment and are pulled in many directions as new projects and priorities continuously emerge. Without systems for follow-through in place, it's very easy to commit this matrix trust buster. To avoid dropping the ball, use calendar prompts, automatic reminders, to-do lists, or any other high- or low-tech solution that will help you be disciplined with your follow-ups.

## A Closed Mind and a Lack of Curiosity

Closed-mindedness can be a subtle trust buster, yet we often hear the criticism in matrixed organizations that a person is unwilling to explore new ideas, and, most relevantly, is not interested in others' priorities. If this is a criticism you've faced, it may simply be that you process things internally and don't ask many questions, that you are preoccupied with other matters that cause you to be less engaged, or that you are focused on getting your perspective across.

However, if you are unable to demonstrate an authentic interest in the perspectives, priorities, and opinions of your matrix peers, you may be impacting trust without realizing it. Why is this subtle behavior so important? Remember the earlier premise of the unique interdependent nature of the matrix: "As I collaborate with my stakeholders, I have to trust that, while they have their own agendas to fulfill, they also care about mine and my thinking." Though it may be a mistaken perception, a stakeholder who repeatedly experiences you as disinterested in the goals of others may conclude that you are only there to advance your agenda and impose your thinking.

*Bad-Mouthing*

Criticizing or belittling others is something we have likely all observed and perhaps even participated in. As human beings, we can become frustrated when we feel pressure to do more with less; when projects appear to be moving slower than they should; when we feel someone is resisting our brilliant thinking; or when others minimize our priority. Welcome to the matrix! While all of these emotions are perfectly understandable, if we allow our frustration to spill out in the form of bad-mouthing via conversation, email, texts, or instant messaging, we can quickly find ourselves in a vicious trust cycle.

In addition, bad-mouthing can itself cause an instant loss of trust with your immediate audience, who may be wondering, "What does he say when I am not in the room?" Resisting this behavior is critical at every level of the organization, but team leaders who disparage others can be particularly damaging. Their behavior sets the tone, and they can reinforce the idea that venting or bad-mouthing a stakeholder (or stakeholder group) is acceptable on the team.

*Disrespectful Communication*

It seems obvious that we should communicate respectfully, yet it's striking how often leaders reveal that the root cause of a conflict was a communication they perceived as disrespectful. The incident or behavior does not have to be dramatic to qualify as a trust buster. It can be as simple as interrupting a person in a meeting more than once or using language that makes people feel defensive or embarrassed. Email communication is a common culprit, as tone can be tricky to interpret in writing; also, differences in communication norms between cultures can lead to words being misunderstood and received as disrespectful (see chapter 9, "Demonstrating Cultural Savvy").

*The Blame Game*

As has been well established in studies on matrix organizations and on collaboration in general, there are tremendous benefits to having stakeholders from different parts of the organization involved in driving the best ideas forward. However, this diversity of stakeholders also means that when projects and initiatives are not going according to plan, it is easy to point fingers at the stakeholder partners we are working with. We have heard countless examples of these dynamics. Few things break trust more quickly than throwing colleagues or partners under the bus.

### Undue Credit

Taking credit for the contributions of others or not sharing credit appropriately is a sensitive issue in the matrix. Different stakeholder groups are frequently involved in a project at different times, and toward the end, some may be forgotten and not invited to the meeting with senior leadership to share the success. Although many leaders profess that they are not interested in the credit, as long as the right outcome was achieved, most people are pretty sensitive if they believe their hard work was not recognized. If they think credit for their contribution was stolen, even if that was nobody's intent, their reaction is even worse. This scenario can unravel trust quickly.

### Mishandling of Information

Information is power and influence, and the way it is used can have a significant impact on trust. Breaking a confidence is one way information can be mishandled. However, the more common trust buster is failure to share information in a consistent and timely way with stakeholders. You read an example of this in our case study, where Ernesto relied on a person he knew from a previous job and didn't understand that he was shutting out others. When leaders find out others received information before they did, they may make assumptions: "Oh, so Cheryl gets special treatment. I wonder what other preferential treatment she gets," or, "I get it, I'm not in the inner circle." If we are not careful about when, with whom, and how we share information, our oversights can easily drive a wedge between people.

*Evasive and Incomplete Communication*

Nothing inspires mistrust more quickly than the sense that you're not getting a straight answer. When an individual communicates in a guarded or incomplete manner, others wonder if that person is not being candid or fully transparent. As a result, attributions of "hidden agendas" and/or lack of transparency can lead to stakeholders responding in kind. As a result, the sharing of information and constructive discourse can quickly disappear.

## Matrix Trust Builders

Now let's look at trust builders, the flip side of our discussion. Building trust is not just about avoiding mistakes or bad behaviors; it is an intentional process designed to promote a positive sense of collaboration and commitment.

*Positive Orientation*

We are not advocating for naivety or blind trust, but it is important to enter matrix stakeholder relationships with a trusting disposition. Adopt a mindset in which you give people the benefit of the doubt rather than jumping immediately to a negative scenario. This sounds much easier than it is. As human beings, we tend to react with anger or fear if someone behaves in a way that is untrustworthy (even if this is just our interpretation). If we don't check this impulse, we find ourselves heading toward a vicious cycle, rationalizing all the way about our shifts in behavior and feeling perfectly justified. The key discipline here is this: When you catch yourself changing your behavior in a way that leads to vicious cycles (bad-mouthing, being less engaged, not sharing information, etc.), stop and reflect on the following questions:

- Which behavior triggered this reaction in me?
- Is it possible that I misunderstood and am jumping to a conclusion too quickly?

- Have I applied my matrix empathy mindset to this scenario? Can the behavior that triggered me be explained in a more benign way?
- Perhaps this is a misunderstanding; is it worth checking to see if the behavior was intended the way I originally interpreted it?

*"Check-In" Discussions*

Checking in is a skill that, if applied appropriately, might head off the majority of vicious cycles. Sadly, we don't check in with others often enough because of our human tendency to allow any behavior we interpret as low trust to take us all the way down the rabbit hole, into a vicious cycle. However, if we use the positive reflections above to catch ourselves, we have the opportunity to stop the vicious cycle in its tracks and, hopefully, continue the virtuous cycle. Below are some helpful phrases to use in a check-in discussion to increase the odds of success:

- "Barbara, if you have a couple of minutes, I wanted to have a quick debrief with you regarding the meeting you facilitated yesterday. It may not have been your intention but when you spent less meeting time on my team's project compared to the others, it raised some questions for me and the team."
- "Jyoti, if you have a few minutes, I would like to discuss the email you sent to the group this morning. I'm guessing it was an oversight, but when you didn't mention my team's contribution to the project, some of my team members had a negative perception."

Checking things out takes primarily courage but also skill. As in the examples above, it can minimize defensiveness to use phrases that communicate good intentions and to give others the benefit of the doubt. Is there some risk that the other person will react defensively or negatively? Sure. However, think of the risk of starting a vicious cycle on a matrix collaboration. The damage that can cause is far greater.

*Accountability*

Follow-through builds trust. Embrace tools that help you keep your word for deadlines and deliverables—make lists, put deadlines on your calendar, and schedule progress checks and updates. You build trust by demonstrating that you are on top of things. Below are some useful tips:

- **Set realistic goals.** Make sure you anticipate potential issues and leave extra time to handle them. It is better to underpromise and overdeliver.
- **Be clear with the scope and expectations.** Make sure everyone understands what they are responsible for and what you will be delivering. Be specific!
- **Don't reinvent the wheel.** Once you find a system that works, keep using it. Don't try something new for each task/project.
- **Share challenges early.** Let people know as early as possible if you feel the task will take longer than expected. Don't be a hero. It's better to be realistic than to disappoint people who are relying on you.
- **Don't be afraid to ask for help.** If you are facing a challenge that is taking up too much of your time, ask others for assistance in resolving it.

*Effective Information Sharing*

The way you communicate will go a long way toward demonstrating that you can be trusted. When sharing information with other stakeholder groups, ask yourself the following question: "Who would I expect to have this information?" Then, make sure those people are looped in. Do your best to distribute information to everyone involved around the same time.

Certainly, there are times when too many cooks crowd the kitchen. Still, you need to discern who does need to be involved in a decision and communicate that clearly. If someone expects to be included but is not, that person may lose trust in you. When more people are involved than necessary, narrow the field of decision makers and let people know so they're not surprised.

Beware of the temptation to withhold information because you feel it may be beneficial to you. For instance, you may think to yourself, "If I don't share this information with Hans from supply chain, that is one less meeting I need to schedule and one less person I need to get on board. Things will progress faster if I just keep this information to myself and move ahead." Also, be careful about casually sharing information with those you are familiar with first. Others may see this as preferential treatment. It is important to be thoughtful about how you share information, with whom, and when.

- **Be timely.** When you can, be quick in communicating. The longer you wait, the more folks might think that any delay was intentional.
- **Communicate openly and transparently.** The more direct and detailed you can be, the more trust your message is going to inspire. People respect those who are candid and transparent, even if the news isn't always good.
- **Be disciplined with your communications.** If accumulated frustration or stress has you in an emotional state that is causing you to be abrupt, hyperbolic, accusatory, or worse, have the discipline to hold your thoughts for the moment. This scenario is a vicious cycle waiting to happen. Another good reason to refrain from communicating until you've calmed down is that you may feel drawn into bad-mouthing the source of your frustration, which can have a trust-busting ripple effect of its own. If you have one trusted partner you can vent with, that is okay, but don't underestimate how easily vicious cycles can get going if you share your frustrations with too many people.
- **Honor confidentiality.** Remember how important it is to protect information told to you in confidence. Whether it is business related or personal, information given to you with the expectation

that it will remain private should not be divulged unless there is a legal or safety reason for doing so. You may find it especially tempting to share juicy details about a colleague, but this can damage your reputation as well as the subject of the gossip. Practice verbal discipline.

### Respectful Communication

Being respectful when you're challenging others and giving your point of view is crucial to maintaining trust in a matrix environment. Be direct and clear but use language that's courteous. The words matter. And consider how you're being heard: How disposed to you and your message is your audience likely to be? Can you frame your thoughts in a way that will make your audience more receptive to what you have to say? In chapter 6, we will provide you with the executive vocabulary you need to hit the trust sweet spot.

### Focus on Learning and Solutions

When things don't go well, focus on fixes and what can be learned for the future rather than assigning blame or pointing fingers. Naturally, if you or your team made mistakes, own them. Holding yourself accountable for a mistake is a powerful trust builder.

### Due Credit

When it comes to giving positive feedback, document, document, document, all through the course of a project. That way, you're less likely to forget who contributed and how. You can do this via group email with appropriate leadership copied or when presenting a success at a senior meeting. And, of course, consider writing a note or making a call to personally recognize an individual who contributed to the project's success in a meaningful way. You'll engender a lot of trust when people know you're paying attention to their contributions.

*Trust Check-Ins*

Share with your team and stakeholders the importance of trust and let them know how easily misunderstandings can occur. Talk about the trust busters you've witnessed in the past and provide some of the trust-building skills we've included in this chapter. Schedule trust check-ins on a regular basis to catch any emerging vicious cycles. Using the framework of virtuous and vicious cycles, conduct these check-ins by setting designated times to reflect on the following actions as a group:

- First, recognizing the importance of maintaining virtuous cycles, let's reflect on the trust practices that have been effective in building and maintaining these positive cycles, if they exist. This way, we can all be clear on behaviors we should continue and potentially do more of.
- Second, knowing that we all believe we are starting with good intentions, but that even with our best efforts we may either behave or interpret behavior in a way that can negatively impact trust, let's reflect on behaviors that may result in moving out of a virtuous cycle, so we can address these.

Make trust check-ins part of the process so they are normal and expected. You might schedule these discussions to take place every other month or during quarterly meetings. Dedicate part of the agenda to checking in on trust, creating opportunities to address any vicious cycles that have emerged or are emerging. Make sure to review the power of trust practices and why they are so important to your team's success.

## REPAIRING TRUST

Can broken trust be repaired? We are asked this question all the time. The answer is yes, but it's not an easy or quick process. For a glimpse into how trust repair works, let's go back to our case study of Ernesto and see what happened.

After the CEO broke up the near fisticuffs in his senior management meeting, he had to step back and figure out what to do next. He spent several hours deliberating about the situation. On one hand, he knew Ernesto had good intentions and the right combination of skill and experience. However, he could see that Ernesto's lack of skill in leading within the matrix would prevent him from being successful at the company. Ernesto's behavior had undermined trust, and the current situation was untenable.

The CEO reached out to Suzanna B., a long-tenured executive with the company who was the country leader for Canada. He asked her to gather specific feedback about Ernesto and to mentor him so he could become as effective a leader at this company as he had been in other organizations. After many interviews with people around the company, Suzanna sat down with Ernesto for a feedback/coaching session.

She said, "Ernesto, I have talked to many people, and almost everyone thinks your intentions are good and that you want to do the best thing for the enterprise and our customers. But even people who think they are acting with integrity and the right intentions can inadvertently do things that can be perceived as untrustworthy."

Suzanna then described the specific actions and mistakes Ernesto had made and, even more important, how they were perceived. She clarified for him the distinction between intention and impact, and he felt like he was beginning to understand how his current difficulties began. Even more important, he felt that, with Suzanna's guidance, he could overcome his poor start at the organization.

What's important is that Ernesto kept an open mind and wanted to understand the mistakes he had made and how he could prevent himself from making similar ones in the future. After meeting with Suzanna, he contacted the people he had upset and apologized, explaining that, while his intentions were good, he had handled things poorly. He asked if they could meet in person to discuss the matter and put it behind them. Ernesto's willingness to own his mistakes and do whatever it took to repair them allowed him to reestablish trust with his colleagues.

A trust breakdown and vicious trust cycle are damaging, but they do not have to be fatal. By embracing trust-building behaviors, a person who has betrayed the trust of another can shift the harmful cycle and repair the breach.

---

### YOUR MATRIX MOMENT: BUILDING AND MAINTAINING TRUST

- In a matrix, even high-integrity leaders inadvertently can negatively impact trust if they are not self-aware.
- Trust is about more than good intentions; in a matrixed world, it is a behavioral discipline.
- Trust is not static. It is moving in the direction of either a virtuous cycle or a vicious one.
- Maintain an appropriate level of "working trust" to benefit from virtuous cycles and minimize vicious cycles.
- Schedule time on a monthly or quarterly basis to evaluate the state of trust on your team as well as with your stakeholder groups as a way to catch any vicious cycles that may have emerged and shift back into a virtuous cycle as quickly as possible.

---

### CREATING YOUR TRUST ACTION PLAN

The matrix—and everything that makes this structure great—depends on trust. The matter is both that simple and that important. But the critical nature of trust in the matrix is easy to underestimate because it seems so obvious. Because trust is based on good values and intentions, most people feel they already have this quality covered. Values and intentions are the easy part; however, to succeed in the matrix, you must elevate trust to a daily practice that is top of mind in every interaction. This is where self-awareness comes into play. Based on the trust busters and builders outlined earlier, consider how you will actively manage trust in your day-to-day interactions in the matrix.

- Knowing your personal tendencies, what potential trust busters might you be vulnerable to committing inadvertently?
- What trust builders do you plan to implement in your own work life?
- If you lead a team, what strategies and practices do you intend to implement to ensure you are collectively creating and maintaining trusted relationships in your matrix organization?
- How will you put these plans into regular practice?
- Do you notice trust-busting behaviors in any of your matrix collaborations? If so, what is your plan to address these issues so you can minimize the impact of the vicious cycle and help create a virtuous cycle?

## A FINAL WORD ON TRUST

Trust has an enormous effect on collaboration, productivity, and innovation in a matrix. However, the practical, day-to-day reality of what makes or breaks this essential component of matrix success is often underestimated and misunderstood. When cooperation breaks down and projects stall, organizations fail to see that the root cause is frequently a vicious cycle created by well-intentioned colleagues who lacked awareness of their behavior's impact.

As a leader, you have the power to build trust or break it. Good intentions are not enough. You need to deliberately foster a climate of trust by employing trust builders (and avoiding trust busters)—remember that, as a leader in the matrix, you can be a thoughtful steward of trust in your organization.

CHAPTER 3

❖

# Networking in the Matrix

N O MATTER HOW MUCH you think you know about networking—
no matter how large your Rolodex, how robust your LinkedIn
connections, and how vast your contacts list—don't skip this chapter.
Networking in the matrix is not the same as networking in a hierarchical organization. The parameters are different and the stakes are much
higher. A weak network in a hierarchical environment hurts you. A
weak network in a matrix environment can undermine the entire purpose of the matrix because strong relationships are so instrumental to
the healthy functioning of the structure. This is why we are devoting an
entire chapter to strategic networking in a highly integrated structure.

The advantages of a strong network have been written about extensively, and for good reason. The benefits of networking in terms of
both career progression and organizational effectiveness are a point
of emphasis in most organizational leadership development programs
and are included in virtually all future-leader curricula. All of which
is to say: The importance of building and developing a network is not
a novel idea.

However, an effective network plays a unique role in matrix leadership. It is critical to ensure your matrix network is both wide and
strategic, because without it you will find it virtually impossible to be
successful over the long term. What's more, the network you amassed
in a hierarchical environment may not translate to a highly integrated
ecosystem because the stakeholders you are relying on now stretch
well beyond the vertical structure. This chapter will help you evaluate

your network through a matrix lens and ensure that you are building the right network for your success, and for the larger matrix in which you operate.

## OUR PHILOSOPHY OF NETWORKING

Before we delve too deeply into our approach and strategies for building a strategic network in a matrix, it is important to establish our foundational assumptions about the individuals you are engaging and the purpose of networking. We appreciate that, depending on individual experiences, value systems, and even cultural backgrounds, the term "network" can have a negative connotation. It can be thought of as an activity pursued mainly by political people trying to further their personal agendas or as "schmoozing" designed to advance one's career. For some, the term has taken on a fluffy or disingenuous quality. Or, as one of our clients described networking: "It's the act of pretending to like your colleagues and superficial small talk." If any of these notions resonate with you, we empathize. Yet, we want to encourage that you stay engaged in this critical activity.

Our first suggestion to make the idea of networking more palatable is this: If the term itself has become charged or tainted for you, discard it and use one that is more neutral. Instead of networking, call this activity *relationship building, connecting, partnering,* or some other term that works for you. Certainly, before you throw out the baby with the bathwater and abandon a networking strategy, review the assumptions we make about networking in the matrix:

1. You and the colleagues you are networking with are high-integrity individuals who care about driving the right agenda forward.
2. One of the primary purposes of the matrix is to leverage the power of colleagues to bring out one another's skills, experience, and expertise. The relationships developed via networking are what enable this potential to be realized.

3. Matrix structures rely on collaboration. Period. Networks are critical enablers of collaboration.
4. Although networking is clearly beneficial to career advancement, our focus is on the way it enables people to be greater catalysts for positive change in their organizations.

## WHY A MATRIX LEADER NEEDS A STRATEGIC NETWORK

Breaking down the reasons a network is so valuable in a matrix is excellent motivation for the "how to network" section that follows.

### Developing Information Sources

A strategic network gets a matrix leader access to critical information. As a result of the increased complexity of the matrix environment (i.e., larger numbers of stakeholders, agendas, priorities, perspectives, cultural norms), one of the most critical components of collaborating and navigating effectively is having the information you need to set yourself up for success. Without complete and accurate information, a matrix leader, however well-intentioned, can have her efforts dramatically stalled. Conversely, the matrix leader who gathers information and leverages it skillfully can stand out as a catalyst for change.

If you have your strategic network in place, you are in a better position to work effectively across functions, geographies, and business units. Remember, you may not be in the day-to-day meetings, common hallways, or even the same physical location as some of your stakeholder groups. Vital discussions, meetings, relationships, and organizational dynamics that you are not naturally exposed to are occurring, and these can have major implications for your ability to collect the right information and skillfully position your ideas to gain alignment. Therefore, showing up to a conference call or matrix meeting with simply your own (albeit well-developed) presentation may not be sufficient to get stakeholder buy-in—you may face important information gaps if you aren't in touch with stakeholders in other areas of the business.

Your network can help clarify the true agendas and priorities of your stakeholders. Your connections attend meetings you do not, so they know the points of emphasis and what that stakeholder is focused on achieving, based on their objectives. They know the hot buttons and pain points. Your network may have information that is critical to understanding power dynamics: Who is really driving decision-making in any one group? Information can give you insights into potential pockets of resistance: Which stakeholders may be stalling or actively pushing back on your efforts? And, perhaps most important, information can direct your actions as they pertain to cultural norms. Most of us are aware that there may be different cultural norms from one geographical region to the next. But are you attuned to the cultural differences that can arise among other groups? In our coaching practice, we have seen cultural norms differ from floor to floor in one office building. The more information you have, the better prepared you will be to consider all the elements and ensure your approach is effective. A strategic network is your newsfeed.

Consider this scenario: Mike, a matrix leader we coached in the past, was sure he had buy-in on a new project he was leading. All necessary parties had been consulted, and in meetings everyone appeared to be on board. But when it came time to execute this new strategy, delays cropped up. Team members missed deadlines and were evasive about the reasons. Mike was stumped. One day he decided to contact John, a colleague he had worked with in the past who now had a position in a different business unit. John was also working with some of Mike's team members on other projects. Mike explained his frustration and asked John if he had heard anything related to the project. Luckily, John had. It turned out that one team member was worried that the project underway would eventually lead to his team being marginalized. His fears, discussed in side conversations with John and not in a public forum, had created a roadblock to the project. Only when Mike received this information from John—that this team member was the point of resistance—was he able to confront the problem. Mike met directly with the concerned team member to discuss his fears. Once that team member was convinced, the project moved forward without issues. But without information from his strategic network, Mike would have been left scratching his head, wondering why his project had stalled.

## Influencing and Collaborating

Influence and collaboration are among the most critical components of leading in the matrix, and these abilities are largely dependent upon a strong strategic network. We have already discussed the information your network can provide to help shape your overall influencing strategy. In addition, to get to alignment in a highly collaborative world, you need both allies and internal advocates.

Allies are the members of your network who will be in meetings and on conference calls where your agenda is discussed and decisions are made. They are naturally far more likely to step up for you, to jump in and support your idea, than colleagues with whom you have not built trusted relationships. Allies are not just nice to have; they are extremely useful in an environment that is based on consensus and depends on collaboration. These parts of your network are major assets.

Then, of course, there is the crown jewel of any professional network, the internal advocate. The internal advocate is from the stakeholder group you are working with and agrees to promote your cause. You've built a strong, trusting relationship with this person, and you've persuaded him or her in a one-on-one meeting that your idea is a good one. You're then in a position to make a request—"Jen, I am thrilled to hear that you are a supporter of this idea. If you feel strongly enough, I have a favor to ask: Would you be open to sharing your thinking about the value of this idea with your peers? To your leadership? To your group?"

The power of internal advocates lies in the fact that people are generally more likely to listen to the suggestion of someone from their function, their business, or their region. Finance folks are more likely to trust finance folks than marketing people and vice versa. Those in the local markets are more likely to listen to someone in their market than to someone from corporate. This is a matter of trust based on historical relationships, and also on the inherent credibility of someone who is from the same world and thus understands the needs of that world. As a result, your internal advocate may have more credibility than you do and get traction more quickly. These advocates become your internal salespeople. They become your drivers. A strong strategic network can earn you both allies and internal advocates.

### Innovation and Sharing Best Practices

One of the primary goals of the matrix is innovation, together with the extension of new ideas and best practices as widely as possible throughout the organization. The aim is to create a broad culture of disruptive and strategic thinking, and then move away from the "hero culture" in which every leader believes he needs to come up with all the novel and brilliant ideas himself.

Instead, the well-functioning matrix supports a commitment to "lift and shift" or "lift and adapt" as many great ideas as possible across the organization so the ideas can be applied, rather than letting every team and function constantly reinvent the wheel. This practice of knowledge sharing promotes cross-functional and enterprise-wide thinking that leads to new and creative solutions. A strategic network is a critical support to the innovation process: With a wide strategic network, you have access to an extraordinary range of perspectives, expertise areas, backgrounds, and experiences, all of which can help you sharpen your thinking about a current problem, encourage you to look at solutions with a wider lens, or, ideally, adopt a cutting-edge solution a person in your network has already implemented in their own work.

### Capitalizing on Time

One complaint we often hear when coaching and working with teams and groups is that certain stakeholder partners simply are not as responsive as our clients would like them to be. They do not meet deadlines. They don't provide the information they committed to. They don't present the data. They don't do their part. As a result, the project stalls. Often, deliverables are delayed simply because time is tight. Time is a resource, and there is never enough of it to go around.

A strong strategic network is one way to battle this common challenge. If you have established strong relationships with individuals, they're far more likely to answer your call. They are more likely to respond to your emails and provide information. And they're more likely to show up at your meetings. Your relationship will provide a natural pull that leads these other stakeholders to prioritize in such a way that they meet your commitments. This advantage cannot be underestimated in this busy world, where nearly everyone would tell you they're overwhelmed. The reality is that people make choices every day about what they focus on. In the matrix, you often don't have the power to dictate others' priorities; you are dependent on your stakeholder groups to concentrate on your needs and give you their time. A strategic network can increase your odds of getting that precious time.

## Conserving Trust

Last but certainly not least, a strategic network can help you maintain virtuous trust cycles and minimize vicious cycles. You're already aware of how extraordinarily important maintaining those virtuous cycles is to success in the matrix. They are foundational but also fragile. We all set out to be disciplined about avoiding trust busters and practicing trust builders. But ultimately we're still human, and others are going to interpret our behavior in ways we didn't intend. It's impossible that we won't sometimes forget things.

If you have developed a strategic network, you have guardians against your mistakes. Say you make a misstep, perhaps on a conference call or in a meeting, and people later begin grumbling that you forgot to mention their priority or you interrupted one of the team members. A member of your strategic network is more likely to step in and say, "Hey, listen, I know Ellen, and she's a good person. I know she cares about what we're doing. We have conversations on a regular basis. I am convinced this was just an oversight. I'm happy to check it out with her, but don't read too much into this." Because that person is in your network, you receive the benefit of the doubt. A virtuous cycle may start right there, when that person talks the group out of descending into a vicious cycle.

## ANALYZING AND EVALUATING
## YOUR MATRIX NETWORK

We've established why it is important to have a strategic network. Now let's look at how to evaluate yours.

### Assessing the Current State of Your Network

The first step in developing a strategic network for the matrix is to look at the network you've already got and put it to what we call *the acid test*. You want to roll out your network and look at it in its entirety. For some, this will mean putting pen to paper. Others may prefer using software. The method doesn't really matter; the key is to take a long, hard look at the full spectrum of your current network.

Why bother with this exercise if you've already got a network in place? The truth is, the network you had in your previous organizational structure may not be adequate in the matrix. Possibly, it is, but you'll need to put it through this evaluative effort before you can be sure. And we suspect you will find you need to strengthen your connections if your network is to rise to the level of a strategic network for the matrix. In the matrix, networks are held to different standards than you may be used to.

### *Quality Trumps Quantity*

In a hierarchical world, raw numbers rule. If you've got more than five hundred connections, one thousand followers, or ten thousand "likes," you may very well be happy with your network. But in the matrix, numbers don't tell the story. Instead, quality reigns. You could have everyone from your organization in your initial network, and they may all be great colleagues—we're not minimizing their overall value as people and as peers. However, when it comes to your matrix network, not everyone is equally important. Some people are more critical for you by virtue of the roles they have, the positions they're in, and the current matrix projects or collaborations you're part of.

In a hierarchical organization, the key stakeholders in your network tend to be more static and consistent, whereas in the matrix, the range of stakeholders you are likely to be working with and the increased complexity of decision-making mean that you must account for dynamic shifts when building your matrix network. Therefore, it's essential to be acutely aware of the folks who are critical to your particular position and projects, and to continuously and strategically build your network.

### Matrix Partnerships Are Always Evolving

The person vital to you right now may be someone you have less interaction with a month from now. An individual you are not partnering with today may be your most important contact tomorrow. The reality is that matrix partnerships often evolve. Change happens frequently across the organization, which means it's necessary to periodically reevaluate the strength of your network. Building a strategic network is a never-ending project.

### Your Old Network May Fall Short

Many leaders we've worked with find their old networks need a matrix update. They have connections built over five or ten years or longer, and these were fashioned to help them in a more vertical structure. Their network may be strong in one line of business, for example, or around a certain function. In a matrix, that type of network isn't as beneficial. Many executives pointed out that, even though they've been in the organization for more than a decade, they have to rebuild their networks after the organizational changes take place.

## The Acid Test

Taking this acid test will determine how much work you need to put into developing your strategic network further.

### Step 1: Putting Your Current Network on Paper

You can use the blank framework on page 61 (figure 3-1) to detail your network connections. If you prefer to use networking software or other technology, that is excellent. Take a few minutes and catalog your current network. Have a high standard for whom you include. Don't catalog everyone you've ever worked with on a project or socialized with at team meetings. Following are some specific criteria for the kinds of interactions that qualify a person as a part of your strategic network rather than as a mere colleague. As you complete your network map, consider these points to ensure you are including the right individuals:

- The person is your ally when you are trying to influence others and get your ideas implemented, and you are her ally as well.
- You are "thought partners," regularly sharing ideas and information with each other to help improve your solutions.
- You support each other by providing valuable insights around stakeholders' priorities and agendas, and around cultural norms.
- You trust the person would speak in positive terms about you and your contributions when you are not in the room, and you would do the same for him.
- You provide each other with feedback and a heads-up if someone misinterprets your behavior in a way that could negatively impact you if not addressed.

### Step 2: Evaluating Your Network

Now that you have a complete view of your current network, evaluate its strength within the matrix context. Below are three key questions to reflect on:

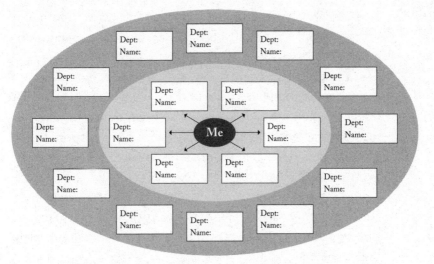

FIG. 3–1 Network Assessment

- **How strong is my network in relationship to my key stakeholder groups?** By definition, if you have moved toward a highly integrated, matrixed structure, you are now partnering with stakeholder groups beyond your own function or business. These groups may be on the same floor of the same building or in a different time zone. Whatever the case, you need to develop your network to ensure that you have relationships with these new stakeholder groups. As you look at your current network, analyze the stakeholder groups that are important to your success. Are there groups in which you don't have a contact who rises to the level of a strategic network connection? From our perspective, this is a potential gap.
- **Is my network balanced?** Next, consider your network for balance of power. Naturally, it is helpful to have in your network the most senior individuals who are part of your important stakeholder groups, but that's not always possible. Don't panic. Individuals at more junior levels on the organizational chart are still very helpful. They're in the meetings. They're part of that culture. Aspire to build your network with senior influencers where

possible, while also ensuring you have a strong network with your peers and, depending on your level, those in more junior positions. Take special note of the balance in your network to confirm that you have connections at all levels—senior, midlevel, and junior. If you notice a place where you do not have a senior leader in your network, consider it an opportunity for improvement. This is true of other levels as well. If your network tips in one direction, develop in the other for balance.

- **Is my network too narrow?** A very important criterion for assessing your network is its breadth. You may look at the network you put on paper and say, "Hey, I've got a pretty good number here and these are all good people, but the majority are part of my team, group, function, business, geography, or building." That is a key observation, as breadth is an important difference between a strategic network in the matrix and an old-school hierarchical network.

  A network that is deep in one area may work for a hierarchical platform but it will fail you in the matrix. The ever-changing nature of the matrix demands that you cultivate an enterprise-wide, cross-functional network that spans businesses, boundaries, and even countries. You may be working on a project now with connections to a particular function. But in twelve to eighteen months, you may be somewhere else entirely. Or the organization may change around you. If you have a narrow network, all your eggs are in one basket, and you are one restructuring or leadership change away from being isolated.

  Having a wide network is a defense strategy that guards you from isolation in a fast-moving and ever-changing environment. It is also a personal strategy of offense. We hear stories all the time about those with a wide network having many more job opportunities. This is a function of engaging and interacting with different parts of the business. If you are in a person's network, she may put your name forward when an opening comes up. If you're coming from another part of the business, you will need that advocate at the table.

## Identifying Your Network Gaps

After reflecting on the questions regarding the strength, balance, and breadth of the ideal network, revisit your original network list. Do any gaps stand out? If so, don't worry; very few leaders start out with an outstanding network. The key is to be aware of opportunities and build a plan. While your results are top of mind, list three to four opportunity areas—these may be specific individuals whose names you already know, or you may simply notice particular stakeholder groups where you are lacking connections (i.e., a leader from the field supply chain). In the next section, we will offer specific strategies for building and maintaining these relationships.

## HOW TO BUILD AND MAINTAIN
## YOUR MATRIX NETWORK

Some of the individuals you are targeting as network additions will already be in your realm; perhaps they are part of your business segment, your division, or your function. Or perhaps they are in the same region or building. These might be the gaps you identified in your acid test as essential to your success. In a certain respect, this group is more straightforward to build relationships with because of their proximity. However, you still need to have a strategy and make them a priority.

In addition, depending on your scope and responsibilities, you may have also identified network gaps you'd like to fill with people who are not in your immediate group or function. They are not in your building or region or even your time zone. These folks are far off your basic networking radar, and yet they are the most important gaps you need to close as you build your strategic network.

These connections are not necessarily easy to make. In our coaching sessions and seminars, this is the point when participants raise their hands and say, "Yes, but how do I do it? How do I build a relationship out of the clear blue sky?" The strategies that follow offer the best potential for success.

## Reach Out for a "Meet and Greet"

Perhaps the biggest hurdle in developing a network is overthinking the initial connection (with a close second being procrastination—we'll address that later). Some leaders, particularly those who are introverted by nature, may spend hours thinking of a reason to justify reaching out. But the gesture can be a straightforward and simple one. In a matrix structure, where relationships are essential, there is either an implicit or an explicit understanding that connecting with new people is a must. Send a well-crafted email to an individual you have identified and share your interest in connecting over coffee—simply say you would like to learn more about him and his experiences and expertise, or that you are looking forward to collaborating with him on an upcoming initiative. If the person does accept your invitation, remember to bring your genuine curiosity. Demonstrating sincere interest can go a long way toward creating a positive relationship going forward. This simple technique of connecting over coffee or lunch can also be an excellent strategy for maintaining your network.

Many of our best networking clients have shared that one of their practices after an initial meet and greet is to suggest follow-up meetings with that person on a quarterly or monthly basis. This way, there is no need to invent a reason each time you want to connect, and you are creating a natural continuity in the relationship. Remember, you have to eat lunch every day anyway, so you may as well make the most of the time. If you currently spend that time either working or surfing the internet, consider designating one lunchtime a week for establishing and maintaining new relationships.

Again, if you find yourself spinning, looking for that perfect reason to reach out, consider the simple solution—just do it! This same advice applies when you are contacting those folks who work in different regions or in parts of the business you don't have a history or organic connection with. Just reach out and be direct and authentic. Here is one example of an introductory networking note:

My name is Jane Smith, and I am reaching out because I am looking forward to partnering with you on the accelerator initiative.

As I have not had an opportunity to partner with you in the past, I would really appreciate it if we could schedule some time so I can learn more about your experience and background. In addition, it would be great to learn more about your thinking as it relates to the project, your top priorities, and any communication preferences you may have so my team and I can best partner with you.

If this approach strikes you as awkward, pause for a moment and reflect on how you would react if a colleague you had not worked with previously reached out to you in this way (we assume you trust the person's sincerity and integrity). Most of our clients have said that they would react positively to this kind of overture.

## Bridge Your Network

Another effective strategy when building your strategic network is asking your existing network for help. When our clients do the network reflection and analysis exercise described above, they often discover that many of their network gaps are in parts of the organization they have not previously partnered with, so they're not familiar with the teams and norms. If reaching out to someone you don't have an organic connection with feels too uncomfortable, consider checking in with your current network to see if someone you know is willing to make an introduction for you.

## Find Things in Common

Take advantage of any networking events your company may offer, such as intranets organized around common interests or ideas. Most organizations today do a terrific job of creating affinity groups, so look for one that resonates with you. One great way to connect with senior leaders is by spending time with them during company-sponsored volunteer days or at company-organized sporting events. Not only can these be excellent openings for a relationship, but you now have a common interest that can keep you engaged over the long term.

## Ask for Help

Asking for help can be a powerful way to both initiate and maintain relationships. Most people are, by nature, helpful, and they enjoy being in a position where they can offer guidance, experience, or expertise in service of the company's mission. Reach out to a peer who has expertise in an area that could assist you, or whose experience can help you develop a more enterprise-wide perspective. If your connection is able to offer you valuable help or information, please remember to give that person due credit!

A request for an opinion or guidance can also be a great way to build your network with senior leaders, the group that is often most daunting to approach. With all the stress and complexity that senior leaders must navigate in their workdays, some of their most meaningful moments come when they are developing talent and helping team members increase their impact and progress in their careers. Reaching out to them with a sincere request like, "I really admire your leadership style and the positive impact you have on the team and our organization. I would appreciate it if you could spare some time to provide me with insights on how I can continue to develop as a leader in the organization." Be patient. It may take several weeks before such a meeting can be scheduled. And if the meeting needs to be rescheduled, don't take it personally. If you do get an opportunity for such a discussion, show up well prepared and ask meaningful questions. We do not recommend questions that focus solely on self-interest, such as, "How do I get promoted?" Instead, ask questions like:

- "What do you consider the critical abilities for our organization's leaders of the future?"
- "What areas do you recommend I develop to increase my impact?"

Finally, if a senior leader does offer you guidance, develop a plan to act on it and follow up. If a high-level executive sees you taking her coaching seriously and acting on her advice, your relationship may develop into a powerful mentorship that stretches far into the future.

## Help Others Without Keeping Score

You also need to be in the category of helpful colleagues who enjoy supporting team members' successes. If this isn't your natural disposition, we encourage you to develop it. Being intentional about ways you can support your connections and anticipating their needs are arguably the most critical facets of this whole strategic networking discussion; in fact, these things are so important that we devote the following section to them. The research is clear: People who don't focus on the quid pro quo and simply orient themselves toward being as helpful as possible are invariably well rewarded.

## NETWORK PARTNERSHIPS

We have laid out the importance of a strategic network and explained how to assess and build it, but we would be remiss if we didn't ensure that you understand how to leverage the network you are investing in. Equally important is that you show up as a great network partner yourself. A great network that you don't use isn't of much value!

## Use Your Network

Check in with your network before meetings to gather critical information that can shape your approach and messaging. As we shared in the opening of this chapter, one of most powerful benefits of the network is its ability to provide you with information that can help you successfully collaborate with and influence matrix stakeholder groups. Whether these insights concern cultural norms, presentation preferences, power dynamics, points of resistance, or priorities and hot buttons, this information can make or break your success. Following are sample questions you may ask your network to glean this information:

- "I am still quite new to your region and would love to avoid any cultural missteps so I engage everyone with the respect they deserve. Can you share with me key dos and don'ts, and perhaps some of the common mistakes you have seen folks from my part of the country make when interacting with your culture?"

- "I am really looking forward to the meeting next Thursday and am in the process of finalizing my presentation. I aim to make my presentation a value-added part of the meeting, and am wondering if you could offer guidance on how to best structure or style my presentation so it is well received."

- "As this is going to be a large meeting and I am pretty new to the group, I was wondering if you could help me understand some of the group dynamics around decision-making norms so I can ensure I am focusing my message skillfully."

- "In the interest of making my presentation relevant to your group, it would be really helpful if you could give me any insights into the highest priorities, or let me know of any hot-button issues to be aware of."

## Cultivate Allies and Internal Advocates

Enlisting the support of your allies and advocates can be instrumental in gaining the alignment you need to move your initiative forward. Here are some ways you might frame these requests:

- "I'm really glad you will be part of the meeting on Tuesday, as we have a common perspective on the right path forward. I know how much the group respects your opinion, so sharing that support, if you are comfortable, would be really helpful."

- "It's great to hear we are on the same page in terms of the best program for your function. It's been my experience that, if your team is still undecided, they will be much more interested in your internal perspective than my external one. I have a favor to ask: If you feel strongly that this is the right way forward, could you share those sentiments with your team?"

## Tap into Your Network Connections to Gain Their Perspective

Your network represents a wealth of knowledge. Perhaps one connection has a best practice he can share with you or can broaden your understanding of a part of the business, while another may offer a fresh perspective based on her experience. But these colleagues will only help you if you ask for their help and are open to learning. Here are some ways to ask others to share their thoughts:

- "This is my first time partnering on a project with operations, and I would like to learn more about the function, current priorities, and trends. You have years of experience and wisdom. If I were to buy you lunch, would you be willing to educate me on some of these topics?"
- "I'm reaching out because I have been really impressed with your presentations and the thoughtfulness and creativity you always bring to them. My team and I are focused on the following problem and I would really appreciate your perspective on it."

## Gain Insight into the Way Stakeholders Perceive You

In chapter 2 we explored the importance of trust and virtuous cycles in a matrix. Unfortunately, many people commit trust busters through unwitting miscommunication. Consider making an agreement with a network connection from a specific stakeholder group you are partnering with: schedule periodic debriefs about the dynamics of the two groups and provide feedback to each other (without being inappropriate or breaching confidences) about any negative perceptions either of you may have created. This way, you can address the matter quickly.

A similar issue that arises frequently in matrix meetings—especially virtual ones—is that two stakeholder groups come away from the meeting with very different understandings of what was agreed to in terms of commitments and next steps. We have seen numerous instances in which the only thing that prevented a complete disconnect, resulting in mutual frustration and conflict, was a network connection reaching out to another and preventing that scenario from happening.

Consider the following example. The supply chain organization of a global technology company is working on an efficiency initiative driven by corporate management in partnership with the global sectors. As a result of the global nature of the project, the majority of meetings took place in a virtual setting, primarily conference calls. Most commonly, the corporate team would be together in a conference at HQ for the calls, while the Asia Pacific team would be together in a conference room in their sector office. During one of these calls, the supply chain leader from corporate was attempting to convince their supply chain partners from the Asia Pacific sector to commit to a particular plan of action moving forward.

Fortunately for the leader from corporate, she had developed a strong relationship with one of her supply chain colleagues in the Asia Pacific sector who was in the room during the conference call. Several hours after the conference call concluded, this network partner from the Asia Pacific office made a phone call to her friend in corporate and shared the following: "I sense that your team believes our meeting ended with us agreeing to move forward, but that is not what happened. Specifically, when you asked if there were any concerns about moving forward and nobody from the other team commented, I sense you assumed this meant they were fully on board and ready to move forward. In fact, when the call ended, several team members on my end shared concerns with one another. It is clear to me that they are not yet fully committed to your plan of action but were reluctant to voice that on the call. I strongly encourage you to reconnect with them one-on-one to ask them about their concerns and provide solutions that will put their minds at ease. Otherwise, I am afraid we are headed toward a lot of frustration on all our parts, with your team feeling that we are stalling and dragging our feet, and our team feeling that your group is trying to push your solution without really listening to our concerns."

## Be a Great Network Partner

We've discussed many of the ways you can benefit from a strategic network but don't forget the other side of the coin: being a great partner to others. You can't expect to gain from your network without offering your help as well. Here are some ways you can become a great network partner:

- Think proactively about information you have that might be helpful to your stakeholders, and offer it (naturally, it must be appropriate to share).
- Consider your relationships and reflect on introductions you could facilitate that would be beneficial to both parties.
- Be willing to share feedback if you see that someone might have a blind spot regarding the way she communicates or is unaware of the way she is perceived by others.
- Go out of your way to share credit and highlight your network's contributions.

## AVOIDING PROCRASTINATION: MAKE NETWORKING A PRIORITY

You have identified stakeholders to focus on and have a number of proven strategies you can use to initiate these relationships; you also have tips on how to leverage your network and be a great network partner. All of this is worth nothing if you don't take the most important step: commit to a plan and put it into action.

As obvious as that statement seems, we see leaders let procrastination or a full schedule get in the way of cultivating the network they need. All too often, leaders tell us some version of, "I developed my network map, identified my stakeholders, and was ready to bring it to fruition . . . and then I got super busy with work and never made it happen." Especially if you are an introverted, task-oriented leader, you may find no activity easier to put off than strategic networking. You may tell yourself, "I know networking is very important, and I will get to it. As soon as I get these urgent deadlines off my plate, I'll begin scheduling those meetings." Sound familiar?

Here is the practical problem with this line of thinking: there are always more urgent deadlines, and the tasks will never be completely off your plate. If you don't change your mindset about developing your network, you will eventually run into a painful reality: When you need the network, it's too late to build it.

Never lose sight of the core truth that strategic networking is a primary element in matrix success, and your network must be wide and active *before* a matrix project emergency hits. When you don't understand why you're not getting a response from stakeholder colleagues, or you go to meetings and feel like you're missing something, it's too late to attempt to instantaneously build your network. At that moment, you can't reach out and say, "Hey, listen, I've been meaning to call you for six months, but I've been busy. I was wondering if you could help me with the following problem?" That will backfire. You'll come across as a jerk networker who is out there with his own agenda.

Many people we've coached have told stories of projects where they've committed a hundred hours to developing a strategy, gathering and analyzing data, and putting together a great PowerPoint deck. Then, they get to the meeting and realize that they haven't spent any time establishing their network. The absence of allies and internal advocates puts them at a disadvantage, and the impact of their presentations suffered because they didn't have the support or information they needed.

What is the solution to procrastination? Develop your network plan, then *schedule* execution, just like you would schedule any other essential project. Obviously, we're not suggesting you suddenly devote 20 percent of your time to networking. In fact, this is where we come full circle to the strategic orientation of this type of networking. It is not a matter of quantity, but of quality. As a result of your reflection and analysis, you have identified the most critical network relationships to focus on. This is how you keep your networking activity manageable and realistic.

Another practical way to ensure you follow through on your strategic networking plans is to find an accountability partner. Share your

---

**YOUR MATRIX MOMENT: NETWORKING**

- Your network is an invaluable resource for success in the matrix organization. It can help you gain critical information, influence and collaborate more effectively, accelerate your agenda, and even build trust.
- The same network that made you successful in a traditional, hierarchical structure will not suffice in a matrix.
- Evaluate your matrix network regularly for its strategic value as changes occur in your role and among your stakeholder groups.
- Remember—when you need your matrix network, it's too late to build it!
- You cannot afford to procrastinate or deprioritize your network—be deliberate about the time you can devote but do develop a plan and execute proactively.

---

networking plan with a trusted colleague, and schedule quarterly or monthly meetings at which you report to each other the progress (or lack thereof) you have made. The more accountability, the better.

## CREATING YOUR NETWORKING
## ACTION PLAN

Building a robust strategic network requires some time and may take you out of your comfort zone, but this investment in your network yields advantages that help you lead effectively in the matrix. There are also immense personal benefits. You can learn an extraordinary amount from interactions with those in your network. You are gaining new knowledge and perspectives, broadening your holistic understanding of the organization, and, of course, dramatically increasing allies, advocates, and sponsors who can help advance your career.

Now it is time to take action! Reflecting on the networking strategies in this chapter, decide how you will apply them in building your network with the individuals you identified as gaps. Articulate a plan that includes specifics, using the following questions and the table below as a guide. Start small, with just three to five people, and add to your outreach gradually over time.

- Who do you need to build and/or strengthen your relationship with?
- How do you plan to approach these people initially? What are you going to say?
- When would be the right time to approach them? Think of a time when they might be less stressed or busy, and thus more open to speaking with you.
- What is your plan to maintain an ongoing relationship with the new people you meet, as well as others in your network? How often should you be meeting with them (weekly, monthly, quarterly, etc.)?

### Networking Plan

| Individual Name | Department/Unit | Networking Strategy | Meeting Frequency |
|---|---|---|---|
|  |  |  |  |
|  |  |  |  |
|  |  |  |  |
|  |  |  |  |
|  |  |  |  |

## A FINAL WORD ON NETWORKING
## IN THE MATRIX

Leaders who invest time and energy in strategic networking are more likely to achieve success in the matrix. No matter how strong you think your network is, there is always more you can do to enhance it so that it serves you well in the unique structure of the matrix.

We have outlined the advantages of a strong and strategic network, and provided you with the tools you need to go out and build it. The key is to start immediately. If you find yourself in need of the network, you may already be too late. Be proactive, and make sure to schedule time to develop connections at all levels of the organization and across a breadth of functional and business groups.

# CHAPTER 4

❖

# Aligning with Stakeholder Priorities

W HAT SEPARATES LEADERS who are catalysts for positive change from those whose impact is limited? The real drivers of the strategic agenda have an ability to influence and collaborate with their stakeholders and build alignment with speed.

You may be the smartest person in any given meeting, and you may have the most brilliant ideas to get ahead of the competition, but if you are not able to convince your matrix partners of the merits of your ideas and get those partners to proceed with your proposals, the net effect is minimal. As we coach leaders in the matrix, we hear a particular set of complaints:

- "It is so much work to get people aligned."
- "It feels like the meetings never end, and it takes so long to gain traction."
- "I'm constantly up against resistance, inflexibility, or ambivalence, or there's an attitude of close-mindedness in the group. They need to be more agile."
- "The matrix is just too difficult. It's too hard to make things happen, to drive decisions. Everything takes too long."

What these leaders are encountering is the challenge of achieving forward progress in the matrix environment, where progress is powered chiefly by influence. You may be thinking to yourself, "Influence and collaboration have always been critical to organizational success, and I've been exercising these muscles my entire career, long before my organization shifted toward a matrix." Naturally, this is true. But there's influencing, and then there's *influencing in the matrix*. It's a distinction many leaders learn the hard way. The approach and skill set you used in the past are likely to be inadequate now as a result of the increased number of variables that impact every situation.

As we shared in the introduction, most of our clients are aware of the exacting nature of the transition from a hierarchical to a matrix structure, and they have taken steps to prepare their organization to meet the demands of this new environment. Following is a recap of the ways most organizations prepare their leaders for the dynamic, highly integrated structure of the matrix.

1. **Develop a change-management strategy.** The transition generally involves a well-thought-out messaging campaign around the need and benefits of the change in organizational structure, communicated in a variety of ways, from global town halls to individual leaders' consistent messaging to their teams. This commitment to change sponsorship is designed to win the hearts and minds of the organization's employees and build positive momentum so that a critical mass of the organization buys in to the new matrix structure.

2. **Introduce new competency models.** These leadership models do a great job of capturing the new competencies and providing useful descriptions of capacities such as: collaborating across boundaries, influencing without authority, driving change, and leading with passion, to name a few.

3. **Clarify roles and decision-making.** Many of our clients have gone to painstaking lengths to create role-clarity documents as well as to train leaders on the latest and best decision-making strategies. These include systems that help identify roles within the decision-making process (decider, informer, etc.), making it

easier to navigate the lack of clear position power when working on matrix projects.

Each of these steps is extremely important for effective collaboration. The skills and strategies we provide in this chapter are not intended to replace the steps, but to complement and build on them. While the preceding steps are necessary, they are not sufficient to help leaders truly thrive in the new environment.

## GENERATING PULL AND AVOIDING PUSHBACK

People do things for their reasons, not yours. That may appear to be a provocative statement. You may think, "What are you suggesting, that my colleagues care only about their personal agendas and not what is in the best interest of the company?" Absolutely not. In fact, throughout this book we make the assumption that you and your stakeholders adhere to certain values and want to do what is right for the organization. However, this does not mean that the laws of human nature no longer apply. Simply put, we all process information from our particular vantage, knowledge base, and biases, and it's impossible for us to do otherwise.

Our reaction to a decision is based in part on the impact it is likely to have on our annual objectives and, yes, our career trajectory. This is not a signal of exaggerated self-interest but rather a completely normal—even healthy—reaction. If your sole focus, when putting together your influencing strategy, is on facts and logic, you may find that your arguments are not wholly persuasive because rational explanations do not necessarily take into account the important components that will sway or influence your stakeholders. You may be presenting a collection of robust data points to support your argument and explain why your idea is best for the organization, but even if you deliver your facts in an inspiring fashion, you may fall short. While it's natural to view the solution through your own lens, your outlook is likely to be skewed by your own position and experiences; instead, you must factor in the way the stakeholders you are trying to influence view the scenario and data points. We are not suggesting that you stint on time when developing a case based on facts, but we encourage you to go beyond pure logic as you plan your influencing strategy. Let's explore in more depth the limits of the wholly facts-based approach in gaining stakeholder support.

## Limitations of Influencing Based on Facts Alone

Conclusions based on facts and logic are not the same for everyone. Just because a particular argument makes sense to you does not mean that your stakeholder groups will have the same assumptions. You amass facts that support your perspective. In the matrix, expect your stakeholders to come to the table with data that reflects their own experience and primary objectives. And even in cases where you can agree on the math, interpretations may vary.

Consider this scenario: We worked with a company that drafted a new transportation process, a plan that leaders were sure would result in a more efficient and streamlined practice based on the facts and logic used to develop it. But when the plan was presented to stakeholders in different global regions, they pushed back on the logic of the proposed change. These stakeholders could agree on the data, but they argued that the data had been examined in a vacuum and failed to account for local contexts such as vendor relationships, history with vendors, and the speed at which potential new vendors could deliver. The same data, applied with different perspectives and agendas, led to different interpretations. The result was a quagmire. Data alone could not generate progress.

The moral of the story is this: Don't count on facts and logic alone to persuade others. Ensure that you understand the perspectives, orientation, and contextual realities of your stakeholder groups. Weaving these elements into your messaging is enormously valuable in increasing your credibility and, therefore, your ability to create the pull you need to move forward.

## Competing Priorities

Similar to differing interpretations of facts, actual or perceived competing priorities often arise in the matrix. While we have no doubt that your agenda and supporting ideas are in the best interest of the organization, in the matrix it is critical to understand how your proposition aligns with and supports the priorities of the stakeholders you are working with, particularly if those agendas appear to conflict. We have witnessed hundreds of leaders who put their ideas forward enthusiastically, assembling impressive lists of the benefits to the company, but missed the reality that these benefits weren't high priorities for the groups they were influencing; in some cases, the proposal actually competed with stated priorities.

One client shared a story that brought this example of "intention versus impact" to life. At a global meeting for a newly formed emerging-markets division of a technology company, the organization's global functional leads were invited to share the global strategy they hoped the leaders in each participating country would embrace. When it came time for the consumer insights leader to present, she passionately shared the new global strategy they were proposing to capture the consumer of the future. In an attempt to punctuate her personal commitment to the success of the new strategy, she ended her presentation by saying, "My end-of-the-year bonus is tied to the successful implementation of this program!" What she did not anticipate was that several of the country business leaders felt that her proposal applied more to developed markets and would not drive success in theirs. Their frustration mounted as her presentation went on, until one of the leaders could not contain his frustration after her closing comment and replied, "Our job is not to help you hit your personal bonus, but rather to ensure that we hit our countries' business targets."

As you might imagine, an uncomfortable conversation ensued. Mistaking the true priorities and agendas of your stakeholders and failing to incorporate them into your influencing strategy can lead to passive or neutral support. It is critical that you convince the stakeholder group that partnering with you and executing your idea will help them achieve *their* priorities. While this sounds like common sense, we can assure you it is not common practice.

## Points of Resistance

In addition to understanding your stakeholders' true priorities, you need to recognize possible points of resistance. And this demand sets up a common paradox in the matrix: the new competency models emphasize the importance of speed, urgency, passion, boldness, and a bias for action, yet in such an environment, nuanced opposition can be overlooked. Every one of the former qualities is essential not only in the matrix but in the world we live in, where events happen quickly and agility is compulsory. Enthusiasm and passion are essential if you are to bring people with you and drive the agenda. However, there is a risk that, in a climate that calls for bold action, you will miss subtle issues that can easily lead to significant resistance.

Excellent leaders who do their best to embody the qualities outlined in competency models bring energy, passion, and vision, but if they miss the resistance bubbling below the surface, they weaken their impact. Time and again, we see great leaders either overlook resistance altogether or do a minimum to address it. That ends up slowing things down. Or worse, their omission can cause the plan to backfire entirely.

As we move through the chapter, we'll address what you as a matrix leader can do to ensure that you are uncovering the human factors that may trip you up. We'll explore the most common issues surrounding resistance and look at ways to overcome them, but first let's examine a case in which resistance was successfully averted.

## CASE STUDY: HEADING OFF RESISTANCE

One of our coaching clients, Jyoti, was VP of global IT architecture for a major consumer products brand. When her company underwent a global matrix restructure, she and a half dozen other IT VPs were dispatched to countries all over the world to partner with local colleagues and implement the new global architecture strategies. Most of Jyoti's IT colleagues struggled to transition to their new roles. They traveled to these company outposts and pretty quickly developed negative reputations as too "ivory tower." They came in with a strong HQ attitude and didn't understand the needs of the regions and countries they were visiting.

But not Jyoti. She managed to develop such a positive reputation with the global partners she worked with that other stakeholders began to request her for their site visits. She was in high demand as a point person for global projects, while her IT colleagues were getting such bad reviews that stakeholders around the globe began to avoid them.

We couldn't pass up the opportunity to ask Jyoti, "What's the secret to your success?" She said it was simple. She understood that, while she was in charge of global strategy and implementing it around the world with these partners, the stakeholders were complex human beings, not just IT professionals:

> When I'm going into any of these stakeholder meetings, I'm of course confident in the quality of our global strategy, and I have all the hard data to demonstrate why it's the right direction forward. But I understand that, beyond this, I'm working with human beings, not robots. I need to take human nature into account. I need to understand their unique business needs and their concerns with the change strategy, and effectively communicate that the outcome will not only be in their best long-term business interest, but that I am here to support them with whatever challenges they will face.

When we asked her to provide more specifics about her approach, she shared the following:

> My first objective when I engage with my global partners is not trying to sell them, but rather to gain a full and complete understanding of what is happening in their country or region

from an IT architecture perspective and the history of how it was developed. It is always essential to respect and acknowledge history before recommending change.

Next, I focus my attention on how the implementation I am going to explore will benefit *their* country or region. Obviously, they need to see the advantages for them. Finally, I listen carefully and look for indicators that may be cause for concern or show reluctance to move ahead. It is my experience that when my stakeholder partners feel fully heard around these important topics, it creates the spirit and dynamic for a real partnership. Then, based on the information I have gathered, I am able to find a win-win solution to move forward. My colleagues have often described our global partners as resistant to change or inflexible . . . my experience is that they are actually quite open-minded if you approach them in a truly collaborative way.

Jyoti embodies much of the synthesis recommend in this chapter. She comes to the table armed with data and logic, but she seeks the genuine enthusiasm and buy-in of stakeholders. To gain that, she looks to understand each stakeholder's agenda and searches for ways to align it with her own. She explores their concerns and resistance areas so she can address them directly. In this way, she is able to influence without authority and bring stakeholders into her vision for the greater good of the company.

It's this confluence—the intersection of empathy and skills—that Jyoti intuitively understands is her best tool. As we continue on with this chapter, we'll examine the ways this can be developed and deployed by matrix leaders. Hopefully, you are now convinced of the importance of understanding your stakeholders' true agendas and priorities (the pull) and points of resistance (the pushback), and the value of using this information to dramatically strengthen your ability to influence and collaborate. In the next section, we'll examine how to discover your stakeholders' true agenda and how to use it as part of your influencing strategy.

## DISCOVERING YOUR STAKEHOLDERS' PRIORITIES AND POINTS OF RESISTANCE

As the sales expression goes, "People will tell you how to sell them." Meaning, if you are curious and resourceful, your stakeholders will often share what is important to them. The question is: What are the key techniques for achieving this?

When you are looking to understand what worries stakeholders or what motivates them, you need the right strategies to uncover the information. These are:

- leveraging your network
- listening carefully
- reading your stakeholder tells

### Leveraging Your Network

We covered the importance of your network extensively in chapter 3, and the detail provided there will help you use your network to best advantage. We encourage you to revisit that chapter if you need a refresher, but we want to emphasize here that you must build your network strategically so it yields important information you can use to understand your stakeholders. Make sure you tap into it to learn your stakeholders' priorities and any possible points of resistance.

### Listening Carefully

Take your listening skills to a new level. Listening for a true (and perhaps hidden) agenda or point of resistance goes beyond asking basic questions, avoiding interrupting, and nodding your head gratuitously during initial meetings while you wait for your turn to pitch. Advanced listening starts with authentic curiosity that puts aside thoughts of selling your own particular project.

We encourage you to cultivate an intention for advanced listening before your first interactions with your stakeholders. Embrace a mindset that asks: What do you (stakeholder partner) know about this initiative from your experience, expertise, and perspective that I don't know? Make no mistake, your stakeholders can tell when your interest is genuine. If they trust your sincerity, which signals to them that you are committed to a mutually beneficial outcome, they are far more likely to be transparent and share their core drivers and concerns. Once you have embraced the ideal listening mindset, ask open-ended questions like these to delve into your stakeholders' viewpoint:

- What is the history around this initiative that I may not be aware of?
- What are your key objectives relating to this initiative?
- What are potential concerns that I may not be aware of?
- When you think about this project's outcomes, what are your success criteria?
- What keeps you up at night regarding the potential rollout?
- If we were to move forward, what would you most like to avoid?

As you listen, be attuned to both facts and feelings. You may ask a question and get a factual answer. But that answer may belie a contrary set of feelings on the part of the stakeholder. Here's an example: As the matrix leader, you propose a project with certain deadlines for implementation and you ask the stakeholders, "Does this work for your team?" The response is: "Absolutely. My team doesn't really need weekends or time with their families. No problem, we can commit to that."

Technically, you got a "Yes, no problem" from that stakeholder. But hopefully you're listening not just to the words but to the feelings beneath them. The tone, if you're listening well and being honest, is that your deadline is not realistic. Your stakeholder doesn't think this deadline is a good idea. That's a point of resistance. Are you listening and addressing the issue or letting the technical answer paper over any disagreement? You need to listen for these throwaways, lines that sound like jokes but in fact represent the stakeholder's true feelings. You're listening to determine the level of congruence in the person's answers; his words may say one thing but his affect and his delivery are saying another.

Even when no words are exchanged, an uncomfortable silence can be a message to the matrix leader. This dynamic can be particularly important on conference calls, when body language and facial expressions are not part of the conversational cues. We were working with a client recently to support a particular matrix project that had stalled. As we conducted stakeholder interviews, it became apparent that a main issue was a disconnect between the groups; one group believed they had alignment and support from the other, only to discover later they had misread the situation. Eventually, we asked the group leader to share with us how he had reached the conclusion that the other group was on board. His answer was very revealing: "It is quite straightforward, really. When we present our information on the conference calls, I assume that if they disagree or have concerns they will ask questions and let me know. If they don't ask any questions, I assume we are on the same page." Hear this: silence is not the same as agreement.

When you pick up subtle cues that point to opposition, your next move as a matrix leader is to take the *unspoken cues* and *speak* them. Here are a couple of examples:

- "Hey, listen, I'm picking up the feeling that you don't think this is a realistic deadline."
- "I'm just curious, do you guys feel like this approach is going to work for your team?"

These types of questions are essential. You are exposing what you suspect are points of resistance. This can be uncomfortable to do, and you may be tempted to just take the yes and move on. But stay in the uncomfortable moment and have the uncomfortable conversation. If you can unearth the points of resistance, you can address them at the onset, which is much easier than dealing with them when they burst from their confines in the middle of the project.

## Reading Stakeholder Tells

In addition to truly listening to stakeholders and engaging your network, your level of awareness in the moment at stakeholder meetings can lead to valuable information. If you are not familiar with the term *tell*, we borrow it from the world of poker. A tell is a verbal or nonverbal behavior (often involuntary or subconscious) that, to the trained eye, provides information about the strength of an opposing player's hand. When cards are being dealt, experienced poker professionals are not looking at their own cards but rather observing the behaviors of their opponents as they inspect theirs. These players are banking on a general truth about human beings: It is very difficult to hide or disguise our emotional reactions.

Poker players are so concerned about revealing a tell that they wear sunglasses in windowless casinos, cover their faces with their hands, wear hoodies to the table, and train for hours to master their perfect "poker face." Here is the good news: It's unlikely that many of your stakeholders are professional poker players. Odds are, stakeholders at your meetings are revealing tells about their levels of interest and enthusiasm as well as points of resistance. The key is to improve your ability to pick up on this valuable information so you can become a more effective influencer and collaborator.

There are two components to effectively utilizing tells. First, you have to able to spot them. Second, you need to respond skillfully in the moment. In this section, we will focus on critical tells that signal two very important emotions: interest and resistance. If we can pick these up, we have an opportunity to react quickly and improve our situation considerably. Here are some tells that signal *interest* from your stakeholders:

- Listeners shift their bodies toward you as you are speaking. You may notice that your stakeholders are maintaining a certain body posture at the beginning of your presentation, but they suddenly lean in your direction as you start on a particular topic.
- Participants shut down any mobile device or laptop they were working on and give you their undivided attention.
- Stakeholders ask multiple questions on a particular subject.

These are all cues that you have just hit on their true points of interest, the areas they care about most. You do not want to miss these signals and just continue with your well-rehearsed PowerPoint deck, or you may miss the "buying signals" your stakeholders are showing you.

If you spot these tells, you are in position to make the most of the situation by saying something like:

- "Since this seems like an area of interest to the group, let me take some time to delve into the data more deeply."
- "I wanted to pause here for a moment and check in. Do you have any questions about the cost-savings initiatives I have summarized here? I appreciate that many of you are seeing this information for the first time, and I want to be sure that I answer your questions."

But not all tells are positive signs. These indicators from stakeholders betray a *lack of interest* in what you are discussing:

- flipping ahead in the deck
- avoiding eye contact and appearing fidgety
- picking up their mobile devices

Watch for these signs and be prepared to move on quickly. You can simply say to the group, "I'm aware of how precious your time is, and I want to make sure I'm focused on what matters most to you. Let me give you a high-level overview of the presentation, and then I'll look for your guidance on where to go into more depth."

## Uncovering Points of Resistance

Human beings also unconsciously reveal when they are concerned or resistant. Beware if you start discussing a topic and stakeholders show the following behaviors:

- leaning back
- folding arms

- breaking eye contact
- looking around the room to gauge others' reactions
- furrowing brows

Any of these can be signals of potential resistance, surprise, or confusion. If you miss these signals and simply continue sharing your perspective, you run the risk of losing the audience as they remain stuck on whatever it was that triggered their reaction. Depending on the context and the audience, you need, at a minimum, to make a mental note to follow up with an individual whose reaction you noticed or to check in with your network to see what may have caused this reaction. If you find that stakeholders have concerns, you can address them at the next opportunity.

The best move, when you note resistance, is to pause and then engage your stakeholders to gain a deeper understanding of their apprehension:

- "I get the sense that what I suggested may have surprised you, is that correct? If so, would you be willing to share your thoughts so I can address any questions you have?"
- "Based on your reaction, I'm wondering if this may be an important point for us to explore further. Are there any concerns you have that would be important for me to address?"

You take some risk in addressing concerns directly in the moment, in that the discussion might be uncomfortable, but if you don't address them and keep going, you are sure to encounter bigger and more frustrating problems down the road.

Finally, while it is true that some people are naturally more intuitive and are in the habit of reading others, this is a skill that anyone can get better at. We encourage you to keep your radar attuned to tells when you attend meetings, as a trove of information is being revealed continuously—this information can make all the difference between effective and ineffective collaboration.

## ENHANCING YOUR INFLUENCING
## AND COLLABORATION STRATEGY

You have learned how to glean valuable insights into your stakeholders' true priorities, agendas, and potential points of resistance, and now comes the payoff! We will break this final section into two parts:

1. Creating pull—Leveraging what you have learned about your stakeholders' true agenda
2. Overcoming resistance—Finding areas where your interests are aligned and learning how to make the most of them

### Creating Pull

In an environment where, frequently, you will not have a position of power over your stakeholders and cannot simply tell them what to do, one of the keys to influencing is to present your ideas in such a compelling way that stakeholders are enthusiastic about getting on board. This is what we mean by generating pull. When you understand the true agenda of your stakeholders, you have the information you need to generate that critical pull. Some examples of a true agenda are:

- short-term revenue generation
- top-line growth
- long-term global strategic objectives
- cost savings and efficiencies
- reduced head count
- talent development
- disruptive thinking

These are only a few of the possible true agenda points your stakeholders may have. And while the best interests of the organization will always be the broad driver, your stakeholders' more specific but less obvious agendas are simultaneously present and, frankly, often more influential. There are two powerful ways to leverage the information you have gathered. First, and perhaps most obviously, rather than focusing your discussion (or presentation) around how your initiative will achieve the benefits you are most interested in, focus on what is most important to your stakeholders. Here is where we come full circle, back to the idea that "people do things for their reasons, not yours."

The second strategy is less intuitive, but the latest research shows it may be even more compelling. In your discussions, highlight how *not* going with your proposal will put one of *their* main objectives at risk. Let them see how declining to support your idea might affect them directly. For example: "I understand that there will be some initial resource constraints if we implement these new processes, but the reality is that if we don't make this investment now, the data clearly shows that our competition will beat us to market by the end of this year."

Fear is a powerful motivator. But again, this technique is only available to you if you know what your stakeholders actually care about!

## Overcoming Resistance

Certain areas of resistance show up with a high level of frequency in the matrix, and you should be aware of these and know how to navigate them. Below, we have described each of these high-frequency areas and provided you with specific tips and strategies for addressing each. As you review these areas and the supporting strategies, engage from a mindset of empathy and curiosity. It is absolutely critical that you establish the right frame of mind if you are to access the behaviors you need to overcome resistance; perhaps more important, an open mindset will create a sense of authenticity and congruence in your interactions with your stakeholders as you aim to minimize their opposition.

### Loss of Control

A common issue in matrix projects revolves around a loss of control, or even a perception that a stakeholder or group is losing autonomy or power. As we've discussed, this shift in dynamics is deliberate, designed to foster greater collaboration and aligned decision-making. However, the fact that the change is purposeful doesn't mean that the benefits are not accompanied by difficulties. Challenges related to loss of control are quite pervasive, so it's a topic we encourage matrix leaders to reflect upon regularly. It would be unusual to encounter a transition to a matrix structure in which no one was fretting over a loss of control.

Concern over losing their power to command is so widespread because it goes directly to the personality of many successful business leaders. Many, many control specialists, as we affectionately call them, end up in leadership positions. These are traditional type A folks who are self-starting, autonomous, and independent by nature. These individuals are happiest when they have been asked to achieve a goal and have the clarity, decision-making rights, and, ideally, autonomy over resources to drive that result. The more they are asked to operate in an environment that is interdependent, where they have to rely on others and where there's ambiguity around decision-making rights, the less psychologically comfortable they become.

As a result, leaders who historically had a sense of control will feel, in the matrix, like they're losing it. That can trigger an emotional reaction and resistance, so it is important to be mindful of this tendency, as it can easily lead to a disinterest in sharing information, disengagement ("if I don't own it, why bother"), anger, frustration, and a lack of collaboration.

There are steps you can take to help a type A individual make the transition to the matrix. If you know (either through personal experience or research) that you're working with a control specialist and you're going to be making a proposal that will take away autonomy, emphasize the parts of the implementation they can control. Show them where they can customize and influence the process. For example, if the change is coming to the delivery process, can your type A be the one to draft the new instructions or manage training?

As with other points of resistance, speak the unspoken. Address the issue at the start rather than waiting for it to fester, using language like: "As the implementation goes forward, we want to work closely with you and make sure that you've got an opportunity to react or provide your influence every step of the way." This doesn't mean you're giving the stakeholder the option of choosing a different strategy; instead, you are engaging this person and asking for input. This will go a long way toward helping that leader feel like he hasn't lost all control.

## A Move from Expert to Novice

Often, matrix leaders are making changes in organizations that have a substantial history. Some of the stakeholders have years of expertise and training behind them. They are professionals used to doing things in a certain way, whether with regard to software, hardware, or a particular set of protocols. Confronted with a situation in which they slip from expert to novice overnight, some leaders may be more than a little unnerved.

As we have discussed, a shift toward a more integrated structure requires new leadership skills. Perhaps in the previous organizational structure, being a subject-matter expert or a technical expert was sufficient, but now the leader is being asked to demonstrate a broader range of skills. As former experts fear they have been diminished, their concern may crystallize into resistance. Their once-prized skills are no longer prized, replaced by a new list of high-value skills that they may not have. This can lead to a spectrum of subtle resistance, which often manifests as passive-agreement head nodding followed by foot dragging or flat out avoidance. Some may hope that "if we just ignore this long enough, things will go back to the way they used to be." Obviously, this type of resistance can stand in the way of progress.

How do you address aversion to these changes? There is no way to sugarcoat this: learning new skills can be challenging, particularly for people who have succeeded for years under the former structure. However, you can mitigate leaders' fears that they will get left behind by:

- emphasizing the support you will provide
- describing the learning resources that exist to help equip them with the new skills they need

These assurances will help those you oversee transition to this new system or way of behaving. It won't eliminate all of their fears, but it will help minimize their concerns and prevent them from simply blocking and resisting.

## Turf Issues

Conflicts over turf were not invented in the matrix structure, and they exist in businesses of all structures and sizes. However, in the matrix, the frequency and impact of turf wrangling tend to be more dramatic because of the interdependent nature of the structure; in a matrix organization, by design, stakeholders outside the division or function are weighing in on the turf of others. The underlying emotions that drive turf issues can be boiled down to: "How could an outsider possibly have more information, more experience, or more expertise in our domain than we do?" This dynamic most commonly manifests as a lack of openness to ideas from stakeholders in different parts of the organization. Such resistance can dramatically stall or block collaboration, undermine synergies and best-practice sharing, and present obstacles to diversity of thought and innovation.

Remember, pride is often a factor here. Stakeholders may rightly say: "Hey, we've been doing things successfully in our part of the company, in our part of the world, and we've done very well. I don't see how somebody from the outside is just going to come in with their amazing best practice or miracle solution when they simply don't understand how things really work here."

And, of course, once a turf battle is in full swing, the "insiders" will give all kinds of reasons that the new proposal can't be done. They will mention their unique consumer base, their special context, their specific environment, and so forth. But often, these points represent emotional resistance to having an outsider come in and tell them what to do.

To address turf battles, you often just need to take the time to sit down and listen. Learn about what's been done in the past and be open to hearing concerns. You need to display authentic curiosity here; others will pick up on it if you are just trying to gain information to make your case. Ask about the group's history, changes that may have occurred over the years, and successes the group has had in order to create a sense of participation and teamwork. Arriving full of criticism about what happened in the past can easily put others on the defensive, even if cooperation is the goal. Instead, communicate that, as a matrix leader, you've come to partner with them and build on the success they've achieved. You want to be respectful of their sense of ownership, their sense of pride, and the ego investment they've likely made. Similar to dealing with control experts, handling turf defenders requires that you look for ways to carve out a balance between their agenda and yours. Look for opportunities for these stakeholders to put their handprint on the initiative.

*Career Trajectory*

Career concerns are an extension of worries about individual performance based on objectives, but the consideration is more than a matter of this year's numbers and this year's bonus. Here, we're looking at ways the matrix challenges long-held plans and projections.

Some large tectonic plates have shifted, and people throughout the organization may feel off balance. Perhaps in the previous structure and in their former roles, before many of these changes were implemented, they felt they had a certain level of status. They had a measure of power within the organization, and they now fear that everything they have worked for is at risk. If the changes that have taken place diminish them, the effects will not be confined to this project or this fiscal year but will impact their careers over the long term.

Furthermore, these people may have concerns (often legitimate ones) that the skills and experience they developed while working in the previous structure will no longer be as valuable in the new structure. This fear is often exacerbated as new hires with the desired skill set come in from more matrixed organizations. These new realities trigger disconcerting questions: "Can I still be successful in this organization? Is my skill set no longer relevant?" Now, the person's career trajectory may not be what she thought it would be. All of these factors can lead people to either consciously or subconsciously push back.

The keys to handling stakeholders' concerns about career trajectory lie in your resources (your network, your listening skills, your understanding of stakeholder tells) and in being prepared with as much information as possible. Individuals' career paths and the way the matrix may affect them is a sensitive topic to broach directly unless you have a long, trust-filled history with the person. Try to draw out the unspoken and bring it forward. Highlight the premium that the company places on leaders who are fully committed to this new way of working collaboratively. Assure them that, while the new structure might appear to diffuse their power or status in the short term, by demonstrating mastery and serving as a model of this new brand of leadership, they will ensure their own career advancement.

As we near the end of our chapter on aligning with stakeholder priorities, keep two realities in mind. First, it is highly unlikely that you will be able to remove all resistance in certain matrix scenarios, but reducing it can make the difference between moving forward and stalling completely. It is worth your time and effort to reassure stakeholders that the new organization, while different and more challenging in some ways, represents a range of exciting possibilities.

You may still find yourself in situations where you have applied these techniques in a sincere effort to be the best empathetic partner, and yet the stakeholders do not budge in their total resistance. In this case, you may have missed the deeper point of resistance and it's worth doing additional information gathering.

Or you may be up against what we call *matrix blockers*—those rare individuals who are truly not interested in collaboration and are instead focused on protecting themselves or driving a personal agenda. For these uncooperative types, you will likely need to elevate the situation to more senior leaders within your organization to gain their support. It is essential to first make a sincere effort to influence and create alignment with holdouts by using the skills we outline in this book. One of the most destructive behaviors to a matrix is the escalation of collaboration challenges at the first sign of difficulty. This not only displays a lack of leadership on your part (which your boss will note), it can lead to unnecessary vicious cycles as your stakeholders come to feel that you are trying to circumvent them rather than partnering with them in good faith. Again, we encourage you to apply all the skills and techniques you have learned, along with your matrix mindset and empathy, to drive matrix projects forward collaboratively.

In those rare scenarios where you run into a matrix blocker, share with your senior leadership the robust collaborative approach you have utilized and where you've become stuck. At that point, it is appropriate for senior leaders to use their power to move things forward.

## CREATING YOUR STAKEHOLDER-INFLUENCING ACTION PLAN

In this chapter we have provided you with the tools to both learn what your stakeholder's priorities are and to leverage that information in your

---

### YOUR MATRIX MOMENT: ALIGNING WITH STAKEHOLDER PRIORITIES

- Figuring out the right technical business decision in the matrix is sometimes the easy part. Getting your stakeholders to commit their time, energy, and resources to those ideas—that is the differentiating skill.
- Facts and logic on their own are often not enough to persuade stakeholders.
- People do things for their reasons, not yours.
- It is essential to discover the true drivers and priorities of your stakeholders. Leverage your network, listen skillfully, and read stakeholder tells—the information is out there.
- Once you understand your stakeholders' priorities, position your message in a way that emphasizes how your idea can help achieve those goals.
- Make sure to uncover any potential points of resistance. Missing "under the surface" points of opposition can derail an entire collaboration. Discovering and addressing them proactively is key to influencing without authority in a matrix.

influencing strategy. Now it is time to take action. Using the skills, tools, and tips you read in this chapter, use the following questions to frame your action plan:

- Who are the stakeholders you need to learn more about? What are their priorities, as well as any potential points of resistance?
- In your previous interactions with these stakeholders (i.e., meetings, calls, company events), did you pick up on any "tells" that could offer some insight into their thinking?
- Does anyone in your network have information about these stakeholders' priorities or points of resistance?
- In your next meeting with the stakeholders, what questions can you ask to help uncover their priorities and/or points of resistance?
- Once you have the information you need, how will you leverage it in your stakeholder-influencing strategy? How can you build on their priorities? How can you minimize their concerns and potential resistance?

## A FINAL WORD ON ALIGNING WITH STAKEHOLDER PRIORITIES

You may be the smartest person in the room, the one with the best ideas, or the one who is most passionate, but that doesn't guarantee you success in advancing your agenda. In the matrix, figuring out the right thing to do from a business perspective may be easier than securing approval to move forward with your idea. If you don't have the skill to influence stakeholders effectively, your ability to execute your ideas will be compromised. By skillfully applying the ideas and methods explored in this chapter, you can dramatically increase the persuasiveness of your message and drive stakeholder buy-in.

CHAPTER 5

❖

# Understanding Power Dynamics

Iɴ ᴛʜɪs ᴄʜᴀᴘᴛᴇʀ, we'll address a rather paradoxical subject that emerges in the matrix: power dynamics. *Power dynamics* refers simply to the way people interact with one another; the reality is that, in any organization, certain individuals have more influence over decisions than others. The theme of power dynamics is a common one because of its significance in developing a successful influencing strategy. Do we understand the chain of command and where power lies, so we can spend time influencing the right people? In the matrix, the importance of power dynamics is often underestimated because, according to the spirit and intention of the matrix, it's not supposed to be a major consideration. The matrix is designed to shift from vertical, top-down decision-making to constructive discourse, creativity, and well-rounded thinking across all experience levels. It's intended to refocus power away from position and toward ideas.

This structural change in matrix decision-making—which is more integrated and collaborative—supports the paradigm shift from vertical to horizontal, but the spirit of the matrix also signals that successfully driving your agenda is no longer about studying the org chart to know who is in power but about skillfully sharing the best of your thinking and influencing without authority. To support this new type of decision-making norm, most organizations acknowledge the potential "power vacuum" created by this style of decision-making and implement decision-making processes to clarify roles and eliminate potential confusion. It may be tempting to believe that, in the matrix, the need to understand power dynamics is a thing of the past.

This is where some matrix leaders run into trouble. While the matrix structure represents a pendulum swing in the direction of collaboration, away from position power and hierarchy, in most organizations, decision-making authority is still concentrated in particular ways. Certain individuals continue to influence decision-making more than others, and certain individuals still have greater access to those decision makers than others. Power dynamics still exist. Therein lies the paradox for matrix leaders: Leading in a matrix is about influencing without authority *and* understanding power dynamics remains critical. With that in mind, the most effective matrix leaders work to influence without authority, but they are simultaneously aware of the true power dynamics in the organization at any given time. While ostensibly contradictory, both these forces are in play.

## EMBRACING THE PARADOX

Making the dual reality of influence and power clear to matrix leaders is a challenge. We often get pushback when we coach leaders, who tell us, "We don't have to worry about power dynamics because we have matrix tools to help us solve any lingering power-dynamic problems. Our organization has worked hard to create decision-making clarity to help navigate the ambiguity. If there are still questions, we utilize tools such as role and responsibility charting systems to help get clarity."

Naturally, we are big proponents of these excellent resources and encourage you to apply them. However, our experience tells us that these structures and resources rarely address fully underlying power configurations and struggles. Far too often, matrix leaders simply don't want to talk about power dynamics. Either they are fully committed to matrix thinking and consider the whole "power" story ancient history ("Why do I need to concern myself with this kind of information? If I just stay focused on the right thing to do, that should be enough influence.") or they're offended we raised the issue, as if, perhaps, we are implying they should focus not on influencing based on the quality of their ideas but rather on political maneuvering.

Of course, that is not at all what we are implying. You should always be focused on the compelling reasons your idea is the right one for the organization, but if you are not aware of where decision-making power ultimately lies and how decisions are made, you may find yourself frustrated. You need to accept that power dynamics exist and embrace this reality as a natural element of any organization. Be mindful of your own resistant reaction that this kind of understanding is necessary only in political environments. Every company, including those with sterling integrity, will feature power dynamics, and certain individuals and/or parts of the business will influence decisions more than others.

For example, in some companies with a long history of matrix leadership, the centers of excellence (COE) hold greater power in decision-making authority than the field businesses. In other instances, the field-business leaders have more decision-making authority. Neither approach is right or wrong, but you must understand what the dynamics are and factor them into your influencing strategies if you want to succeed. Many well-intentioned leaders have spent countless hours putting together compelling narratives and presentations to support their ideas, but because they didn't fully understand where decision-making power lay, they failed to include key people in their influencing approach.

Recognizing power dynamics and dealing with them in an up-front and strategic way is necessary in the matrix. Although we all strive for a fully collaborative process, ignoring the role of power dynamics is a risk no matrix leader should take. Let's look now at how one matrix leader embraced this paradox.

## CASE STUDY: MATRIX LEADERS AND POWER DYNAMICS

A Fortune 100 global company we worked with in the past had undergone an organization-wide transformation toward a heavily matrixed structure over a five-year period. One section of the company particularly transformed was corporate IT solutions.

Before the recent restructure, the IT solutions group was divided in two, reporting to two different leaders. One group was the business-facing group—while they were technically part of the central IT solutions group, their primary stakeholders (and those who most influenced their success) were the business stakeholders whose leadership teams they were a part of. The second group held the technical experts who would ultimately design and execute solutions. Also within this second group were the IT solutions leaders whose core constituents were the functional groups such as supply chain, finance, operations, R&D, and quality.

As one would expect, conflict and tension between these two groups was not uncommon. The business-facing group was under tremendous pressure to drive business results in the short term. The business group wanted IT solutions that helped them solve immediate business challenges and offered highly customized solutions that met the specific needs of their division or business segment. The functional groups, on the other hand, were looking for long-term, future-focused, globally consistent solutions to drive a comprehensive set of IT strategies that would set the company up for long-term success.

As part of their ongoing matrixed restructuring initiative, a new executive, Sally F., was brought in to lead the now-collective IT solutions team. The structure changed so that the two previously separate groups were now the same team, reporting to Sally. Her first objective was to get these two subgroups—the business-facing group and the technical/functional-focused group—to work together as a cohesive unit.

The purpose and objective of the new team was clear: provide leading-edge IT solutions to support current business success, *while at the same time* enabling the longer term, future-focused, and transformational agenda of the functional teams, thus ensuring sustainable growth and long-term organizational success.

After some excellent work by Sally to rebuild trust among the team members and to help them align with the broader strategy, she and her team used a series of skills and strategies to navigate the complex matrix they now inhabited. But her work was not complete. Although her internal team was now aligned, the dilemma of competing priorities between the business and functional teams remained. Leaders within the team felt they were in a lose-lose situation. Sally had some concerns: "If we advocate for and commit to the requests of the division and business leaders, the functional leaders will be really upset and feel we have abandoned them. On the other hand, if we push forward the functional agenda, the business leaders will be upset and accuse us of blocking their ability to achieve business results, which they are quick to remind us should be the entire purpose of support groups like the IT solutions team!"

If the natural tension between these stakeholder groups was not making life interesting enough, there was also a clear difference in power dynamics between these two stakeholder groups. Historically, most of the decision-making authority at this company was held by the functional groups. However, at this moment in time, with the business struggling, decision-making power had shifted toward the business leaders. In fact, the funding decisions for IT projects were made primarily by the business leaders. Furthermore, a particular leader heading up one of the global business segments influenced funding to a greater degree than anyone else, and this leader had a certain group of individuals with whom he had strong relationships based on decades of history.

But while that individual held sway in the business groups, Sally reported directly to an executive vice president who oversaw the functional groups. And this EVP made it clear to Sally that the primary success criteria of her new role were based on her ability to drive a transformational strategic IT agenda with a focus on long-term organizational objectives, not by knee-jerk reactions and short-term-oriented initiatives driven by the business.

To summarize, Sally and her team needed to achieve the following to best serve their organization's success:

1. Work in an aligned and cohesive way as a team even when they may be asked to advocate for apparently competing agendas.
2. Successfully engage with two stakeholder groups that seemed to have different core priorities (even though, of course, both genuinely felt as if they were only interested in the success of the organization).

3. Achieve all of this amid complex power dynamics where the primary decision-making power lies with the business leaders although Sally, and by extension her team, reported to a functional leader.

Fortunately, Sally was highly skilled in developing trust and cohesion within her team, understood how to collaborate with her stakeholder groups, and had great awareness and skill at navigating the power dynamics. We will revisit Sally and learn how she applied her understanding of power dynamics to navigate the team's dilemmas later in this chapter.

## WHAT LEADERS MUST UNDERSTAND ABOUT POWER DYNAMICS

You need to consider multiple factors as you look to understand the power dynamics within your organization. If you do not spend the necessary time working through the following questions, you will surely miss out on the critical information you need to effectively influence your key stakeholders.

### Who Do You Need to Include?

As our IT solutions case study illustrates, it is important to understand not only where decision-making authority lies, but who, specifically, within those groups influences decisions. Determining this is not always as straightforward as consulting an organizational chart. A person may have gained influence as the result of relationships established over time. Many frustrated matrix leaders have discovered (often when it was too late) that they were not influencing and engaging all the "right" people. In some cases, this led to an initiative getting stalled or even blocked because an influential person (whose influence wasn't obvious) was irritated that he hadn't been consulted.

That happens far more often than anyone cares to admit. One executive we worked with told us this story: He had been sent to connect with a particular regional group and help them evaluate their product-investment strategy. He had been very intentional about considering all of his counterparts and the key stakeholders he assumed were the decision makers, spending time with them in their region, gaining their input, and sharing information with them in a timely fashion. However, when it came time to get final buy-in on the strategy and decide to move the initiative forward, these stakeholders seemed reluctant to commit. Although they didn't provide fact-based reasons for their resistance, they offered comments like, "I'm just not sure if the timing is right," or, "Perhaps we should give it more time and gather additional data."

Stymied and unsure as to why, this executive tapped his network and contacted an old colleague who had worked in the region recently. After listening, his colleague was able to demystify the situation: "It sounds like you didn't reach out to Charles, the commercial VP. Even though he is not directly on the team you engaged, Charles has tremendous influence over what decisions get made in the region when it comes to product investment. I have seen it in the past. If he is not engaged directly and made part of the decision-making process, decisions can slow down in a hurry."

## Where Are Decisions Really Made?

In addition to understanding which individuals might have a bearing on decisions, it pays to understand the historical decision-making norms in the particular stakeholder group you are working with. Even as the organizational structure formally changes, long-standing traditions can continue to inform the way decisions are made. These norms can be quite different depending on the business, functional group, or geography. For instance, was the decision-making norm traditionally more top-down and hierarchical within the group? Or was it more collaborative, with all team members expecting to be part of the decision-making process? This knowledge is important when seeking to understand norms that vary by country, but it's also possible to see norms vary between two floors in the same building.

One norm that's crucial to understand is this: Are decisions made at the meeting, or at the "meeting before the meeting"? A leader we worked with shared her story of moving from a large pharmaceutical company where decisions were made during meetings to a consumer goods firm where the real decision-making happened before the formal meeting ever took place. In her words: "I remember going to meetings for the first several months fully prepared with my thoughts, how I intended to gain alignment and even anticipating pushback I might encounter, but it always felt like the engagement was fairly lackluster and that most people's minds were made up. I never felt like I had much success trying to influence. It wasn't until months into the role that someone educated me that by the time the formal meeting took place, 80 percent of the decision-making had already happened."

Do your homework and have this backdrop of information going in; otherwise, you will become frustrated as you misunderstand the true process of decision-making.

## How Does Change Within the Organization Impact Decision-Making?

Living in a world where the rate of change will never be as slow as it is today, another critical area of insight is knowing when power dynamics and decision-making authority shift due to change in the organization. A common question we ask our audiences during our matrix training program is, "Has anyone experienced a change in leadership or organizational structure in the last two years?" Perhaps ten years ago, half the group would answer "yes." Fast-forward to today, and over 90 percent of the hands go up when we ask this question. When we probe further to see if anyone has experienced these changes in the past eighteen months, twelve months, or even six months, we have a critical mass of the room with hands still in the air.

We are living in an era of rapid change, and that fact is not going away anytime soon. As a matrix leader, you need to understand the powerful implications of organizational changes, especially as they relate to power dynamics. How has the structural shift or leadership change impacted power dynamics, decision-making norms, inner circles, and priorities? Many leaders we have worked with learned the hard way that they had not picked up on the implications of change quickly enough and were operating on outdated power dynamics and decision-making norms—to their own peril.

## HOW TO GAIN INFORMATION ABOUT POWER DYNAMICS

The first and most important part of navigating power dynamics is information. Do you know what you need to know?

Very simply, test your knowledge by reviewing your power dynamics checklist. To shift this from an abstract exercise to a tangible one, consider a current matrix collaboration you are part of and reflect on this real-time scenario.

### Power Dynamics Checklist

| Reflection | Answers |
| --- | --- |
| Which stakeholders influence decisions most? | |
| Who influences and has access to the decision makers? | |
| What are the key networks within your stakeholder groups? | |
| How are decisions made (top down, collaborative, consensus driven, at the meeting, before the meeting)? | |
| Have there been any changes in leadership or org structure that might influence decision authority and norms? | |

If you can answer all of these questions with confidence, give yourself a pat on the back. If you discover gaps in your understanding of power dynamics, know that there are ways to fill them.

## Connect with Your Network

As with many matrix challenges, the solution is tapping your network, which can serve as your channel to missing information. If you don't immediately see power dynamics at work, chances are that someone else does. Think back to our earlier example, in which our executive did not include Charles the commercial VP in the decision-making process. This executive didn't understand who was wielding the power, but his former colleague did. The key is to proactively find the influential person before your work is blocked rather than waiting for a crisis to inspire you to reach out.

Leverage your network early. If you're not seeing the power dynamics at work, it's likely because you're not in the room where they are happening. If that is the case, you need the help of someone who is. You have to overcome your hurdle of not being in the right room, group, physical location, or region by finding someone who can get you the information. Our executive in the story tapped an old colleague for help. Build on his example and reach out to your former colleagues before you go into a new situation.

If you are contacting people with whom you have a good, close relationship, the conversation should be fairly simple. But suppose the person you are reaching out to is not a longtime friend but a professional colleague, a person who might help you if you ask in the right way. In this situation, you want to be sure you are asking the appropriate questions. Here are some examples:

- "My objective is to ensure I am fully inclusive in my collaborative approach, and I want to ensure I engage all of the key individuals. Do you have any insights for me? Any suggestions about who I should include?"

- "I have studied the company's org chart and have that top of mind to ensure I am engaging all of the stakeholders I imagine will be part of the decision-making process. Do you have any advice about anyone who may not be obvious that I should get input from?"
- "My experience has been that every part of the organization has a slightly different decision-making process or norm. I would really appreciate any guidance you could provide me on how to best approach your team."

That's the straightforward way—reach out to your network, ask the right questions, and be open about the information you seek.

## Reading Tells of Power Dynamics

There are more subtle ways to learn about power dynamics than asking your network. To explore these, we revisit the skill of reading stakeholder tells. Tremendous amounts of information related to power dynamics are on display when you engage with your stakeholders; you just have to look for it.

- **In-person meetings.** Where do people sit in the room, in relationship to senior leadership? Who do people look at after a question is asked or a comment is made? Who is familiar with whom, expressed by informal interactions and even physically touching? Who do people spend time with on breaks? Who is comfortable interrupting each other? Who seems to defer to another?
- **Virtual meetings.** Watch for "live meeting" dynamics that play out on technology platforms such as web-based meetings. Who are individuals looking at when another is speaking? Where are the relationships? It is important to pick up these power tells in virtual meetings when the software allows you to observe stakeholders.
- **Conference calls.** You don't have the benefit of watching eyes and other physical movements on a phone call, but there's still

much to learn. Pay attention to who speaks most often, who stays quiet, and who is comfortable interrupting or talking over another participant.

- **Emails.** Don't just read the text; pay attention to other clues. Who is copied and who is left off? Who replies or forwards the email?

Keep this list of power dynamics tells top of mind the next time you go to a meeting or get on a conference call. Be intentional. Make notes about what you notice and learn, so you can be that much more informed about the power dynamics of the group when you go into your next meeting.

## HANDLING POWER DYNAMICS WITH SKILL

Once you have collected the information you need, you're ready to position yourself to advantage. Use the intelligence you've gathered to cultivate the right people at the right time and move your agenda forward.

### Get the Right Stakeholders Involved Early

Your first move is to ensure that you have engaged all key decision makers early, providing them with the relevant information and listening carefully to their perspective. Few things can disengage key decision makers more quickly than a belief that you don't value their input. We know this firsthand from our research into matrix leadership development programs. We've conducted hundreds of interviews with senior leaders and key decision makers, and we often hear comments like the following:

- "They present their recommendations for my business, when really it seems like their solution is nearly completely designed. They think they are 'collaborating' with us when they present a nearly fully baked solution. They try to make it seem like they are looking to gain our 'input' on it. And they call us resistant because we are spending time challenging the approach they came up with."

- "We are working so hard to add value, help them save money and time in their business by offering best practices and synergies, and pointing to potential cost savings. But they seem so late to loop us in and share what they are trying to accomplish. It's like they only engage us in the process once they have pretty much made up their minds what will work for them and what will not. It's frustrating."

To avoid reactions like these, reach out to stakeholders as early as possible. Invite them to offer their input and make sure their voices are heard. This can go a long way toward building support and creating a sense among these important participants that they have skin in the game.

## Be Present Where the Decisions Really Get Made

Base your next steps on what you've learned. If you know you are partnering with an organization that makes its decisions at the meeting before the meeting, plan your approach accordingly—loop in key decision makers well before the scheduled meeting and be sure to attend (or ask an ally or internal advocate to attend) the smaller meetings in the lead-up to the final decision.

## Pay Attention to New Leadership

When leadership changes occur, pause and spend some time reflecting on what you know about the new leader's style and decision-making preferences. Perhaps you will now be working with a leader well known for her speed and urgency, compared with the previous leader, known for his measured, risk-averse, and consensus-building approach. You want to match your approach to the new leader's taste for speed, directness, and risk-taking. Adapting preemptively keeps you one step ahead of the power dynamics shift that is surely at work.

Consider as well what new leadership might mean for other stakeholders you deal with. Ask yourself, "Does this change tell me something or demonstrate a trend of power shifting from one part of the organization to another?" A new general manager from the business side could signal that decision-making power is moving from the functions to the business.

Think also about the new leader's inner circle and the trusted advisors who get a lot of time with this new leader. Who are these people, and how well are you connected to them?

Constantly evaluate and reevaluate your network in light of shifting power dynamics. Perhaps your current network was well positioned with the previous org structure or leadership, but with new leadership you may have some work to do. Refer to the network assessment in chapter 3 and go to work! The more quickly you build your network to align with the new leadership or structure, the better positioned you will be.

## CASE STUDY RESOLUTION: NEGOTIATING COMPLEX POWER DYNAMICS

Let's see how Sally and her matrixed IT team met the challenges inherent in satisfying diverse stakeholders. Understanding that the business leaders had a great deal of decision-making authority over the IT projects that would be funded, Sally and her team took a number of steps to engage each of their stakeholder groups:

- They mapped out the business and divisional leaders who had the most decision-making authority. They also noted the trusted relationships those business leaders had and who influenced decision-making authority within each of the business groups.
- They created a team strategy to ensure that they were developing strong, trusted relationships with these key decision makers and with those in the decision makers' inner circles to ensure the team was well positioned.
- They studied the decision-making norms within each of the business groups and structured their approach accordingly. In

particular, they learned that, while the organization was generally collaborative, there was a specific leader who garnered a disproportionate amount of respect and, therefore, influenced many decisions. As a result, Sally made it a priority to spend ample time engaged with this leader to develop a strong bond and gain a deep understanding of what drove his thinking. During her time with him she also sought to have him "shape" the development of the IT solutions team's business strategy early in the process.

- They made it a priority to build strong relationships with the functional teams to ensure trust remained steady, knowing there would be a predictable amount of frustration among the functional teams because they had less decision-making authority. The IT solutions team anticipated that the functional groups might react poorly to this difference in decision-making power and perceive that the solutions group was not advocating on their behalf; therefore, the IT team went out of their way to meet the functional groups' needs whenever possible.

---

### YOUR MATRIX MOMENT: UNDERSTANDING POWER DYNAMICS

- Embrace the reality that, even in a matrix structure, power dynamics exist within your organization.
- Devote some time to learning how the power dynamics work in your organization. How are decisions made? Who has access to and influence with decision makers?
- Gain this information by leveraging your network. Read the tells of power dynamics in meetings.
- Once you understand how power works, design your influencing strategy around the key norms and players to ensure that you move your agenda forward.

---

As a result, Sally was able to position the newly combined IT team as one that functioned well in the matrix, and she was able to secure the buy-in and resource support necessary to execute its plans. This success was due largely to her savvy negotiation of the power dynamics surrounding the IT process. By perceiving and addressing the power issues among the stakeholder groups, Sally was able to ensure that the matrix achieved its larger goals.

## CREATING YOUR POWER DYNAMICS ACTION PLAN

As you can see, power dynamics is an area you can ill afford to ignore. To form your action plan for interpreting the interactions among stakeholders in your organization, answer these questions:

- Can you reach out to people in your network to learn more about the power dynamics in your organization/department/division? What is your plan to bring up this topic? What questions will you ask?
- In upcoming meetings and/or calls, what are some tells you will be looking for? Have you picked up on any to date?
- Once you've gathered this information, how can you leverage it in order to:
  - Get the right stakeholders involved early?
  - Be present when decisions get made?
  - Handle new leadership changes?

## A FINAL WORD ABOUT POWER DYNAMICS

Power dynamics exist, even within your newly matrixed organization. The sooner you embrace this reality and understand how decisions actually get made, the sooner you will be able to leverage that information and influence more effectively. It's important to remember that gaining information about power dynamics is only half the battle. Make sure to leverage that information to align stakeholders and advance your agenda.

# CHAPTER 6

❖

# Honing Advanced Communication Skills

COMMUNICATION IS AN ELEMENT that sounds simple enough, but in the matrix, it takes on a new level of complexity that can stymie even the most experienced leaders. Consider the following scenario: As a talented soccer player in a Division 2 league, you are great at all aspects of the game, including passing, shooting, dribbling, and defense. Year after year, you are selected to the all-star team and considered one of the league's top players. The game almost feels easy. Now, think about what would happen if you were plucked from your Division 2 professional team and dropped into the finals of the World Cup. How would you fare? The game is the same. The skills and techniques are essentially the same. However, the level of play is completely different. The speed, the power, and the intensity have all increased, and as a result, your current ability is not sufficient. The World Cup players' range of skills, precision in passing, finesse, and power are next level. While you may have been a star in your Division 2 league, your skills are nowhere near the level needed to survive, let alone thrive, in a World Cup final.

This is the contrast we draw when we talk to leaders about the challenges of communicating in a matrix environment. Most leaders fail to appreciate the skill they need to be successful in the matrix compared with the level of skill required in a more traditional hierarchy. The majority of leaders think they know how to communicate—and if they were still operating in a traditional structure, they'd likely be right.

However, the clarity and efficiency that may have served them well in the old system are underdeveloped for the new matrix environment.

It's not that leaders fail to see the crucial role communication plays in matrix success. As we have mentioned, organizations generally do a terrific job of developing competency models designed to illustrate and articulate the essential new skill sets, and communication is at the core. Competency descriptors highlight abilities such as:

- facilitating healthy debate
- encouraging diversity of thought
- communicating with passion and confidence

These all call for communication skills. But, we argue, not *ordinary* communication skills. They call for *advanced* communications skills. And without that expertise, demands for collaboration, passion, and innovation will fall flat, landing without impact on the organization.

In this chapter, we'll look more closely at the role communication plays in the matrix and at why advanced skills are critically important. We'll also recommend specific ways to build those advanced skills. Let's examine some of the reasons communication excellence is so essential to collaborating and influencing in the matrix.

## A VICIOUS CYCLE IS ONLY A PHRASE AWAY

A vicious trust cycle may be as little a one word away. In chapter 2, we talked about how fragile virtuous cycles can be and how easily we slip into vicious ones. What derails a virtuous cycle of trust? In many cases, it's as simple as a poorly chosen word or phrase. You may be delivering your report on a conference call, confident that you are communicating effectively. But when you choose the wrong word or phrase—you may not even notice it happening—your message can land like a brick tossed into your machinery.

Consider this example: You're on a conference call with global stakeholders regarding a shift to a new vendor. The change will impact the day-to-day work of everyone on the call. You carefully lay out the reasons for the change, the potential for upside, and the strategy the change will support. You come to the end of the call and say, "So, as you can all see, this is a no-brainer. It really is the only way to go." Your intent is to communicate your high level of confidence and enthusiasm for your solution. But on the other end of the call, time zones away, a stakeholder has heard that phrase differently. She thinks it indicates your lack of openness to her thinking and input, and she sees it as an indication you are not collaborative. As the call winds down, she is already texting her coworkers about her concern that this move is not necessarily the best idea for the broader team and that you are pushing this solution aggressively. Back at your desk, you may have no clue this has happened, but your trust cycle has shifted from virtuous to vicious. Being highly selective in your word choice is of the utmost importance. It's not enough to have good intent; you need the skill to deliver your message in a way that the impact is congruent with your intent.

## IDENTIFYING NEXT-LEVEL MATRIX COMMUNICATION ABILITIES

In the chapter introduction, we used a soccer analogy to demonstrate that transitioning to a matrix requires an overall elevation and enhancement of communication skills. The following sections describe the critical abilities you need to develop for matrix success.

### Influencing Without Authority

Naturally, even in hierarchical structures, you needed to influence your stakeholders. However, there were generally fewer stakeholders, and there was usually a clearly defined power structure that would drive decisions quickly if needed. In the matrix, there are far more stakeholders to influence and, by design, the organization is less hierarchical.

Many stakeholders collaborating on projects in the matrix do not have reporting structures in common. Instead of having the power of a position that allows you to advance your agenda yourself, you now need to rely on your communication skills to do so. And that is much harder. You must balance passion, confidence, and conviction while still coming across as collaborative. If you are too tentative in sharing your ideas, you may not demonstrate the requisite passion that will inspire others to come along. But if you use language that might be construed as too assertive, your words brand you as "not collaborative" or "not open-minded," which can shut conversations down. Remember, in a collaborative context, people don't like to feel they are being told what to do. Your communication skills must solicit buy-in, not demand obedience.

## Creating a Win-Win Situation

In a complex discussion, there may be multiple and potentially competing agendas. Such a situation can easily spiral into us vs. them antagonism. You need to communicate deftly in order to move events toward a scenario in which every party walks away feeling like it won; or, at the very least, you need to successfully blend agendas so that participants feel as though they are all on the same team.

## Managing Healthy Debate

Debate is vitally important in the matrix world, and the matrix is truly designed for active deliberation. The ability to challenge one another's ideas, facilitating a dynamic discussion while keeping the conversation on track and preserving everyone's feelings, sets the matrix on its virtuous path.

Fostering vigorous but respectful dialogue is an advanced skill because it is so easy to send a debate off the rails. We can do it with a wrong phrase. We can do it with a wrong word. We can do with just a wrong tone. If we are too harsh or use language that puts people on the defensive, we've derailed the debate. Deploying phrases like, "that will never work" or "here is the problem with that" or "we've tried that" may be all it takes. Then you're likely to get into a trust-busting rut based on some people's feelings that they've been disrespected or shut down.

Of course, avoidance—failing to challenge others' ideas—is in many ways an even greater risk. When teammates stay silent and steer clear of debate, those people leading discussions may walk away with false assumptions of alignment. Passive-aggressive behavior and other disruptive conduct can follow and may be equally damaging to matrix collaborations.

## Navigating Culture Issues

Some cultures are more direct than others, and it is easy to inadvertently use language that is harsh or offensive and upset a colleague. Conversely, it is possible to be too indirect and risk having colleagues misread key indicators. In a matrix, a subtle but essential success factor is the range, nuance, and sophistication that a leader brings to communication; true masters are able to communicate in a way that gives them optimal impact in any given circumstance.

Given all these pressures, matrix leaders need to prioritize developing critical communication skills to calibrate their impact and ensure their message hits the appropriate mark—and also to navigate the complexity of multiple agendas and priorities. Matrix leaders must be able to read their impact in the moment, pivot when necessary, and challenge the thinking of other stakeholders, all without offending or underselling. Ultimately, the goal is to communicate in a way that conveys confidence and signals collaboration. This is true for meetings, conference calls, emails, and even hallway conversations.

Next, we'll look at a case study that highlights communication challenges. Then, we'll break advanced communication strategies into key sections so you can see how they're executed and how you can use them yourself. All the phrases and words we offer here have been field-tested hundreds of times by leaders in global businesses. You don't have to invent the right words or phrases; you just need to practice them, keep them in your mental file, and know when to deploy them.

## CASE STUDY: FAILURE TO COMMUNICATE

We were called in to consult with a global company whose Moscow marketing team was working with its UK marketing team. The two teams had been collaborating on a project over a period of three or four months. The dynamic had gotten so bad that HR intervened and ultimately called us to see if we could help resolve the conflict.

This clash was a perfect example of what happens when there is a lack of awareness and poor communication on both sides. The Russian marketing team had a very direct and task-oriented approach, together with a communication style that was often openly challenging. Members of the British team would sit down at the meeting or join the call, only to be startled when one of the Russian participants launched immediately into the first item on the agenda. No hello? No smattering of small talk before the meeting got underway? The absence of niceties struck the British as brusque, even borderline rude.

Additionally, the Russians were comfortable challenging their colleagues' perspectives in what was perceived as a harsh and abrupt manner. "Everything I say invites a challenge," complained one British team member. "No sooner are the words out of my mouth than one of them will be in attack mode—'What does this mean? What are you trying to say? What more can you tell me about this?'—I am under fire."

Finally, the British were put off with what they felt was a very "telling" and non-collaborative way of sharing ideas. The Russian team was likely to use words like "should," "must," or "need to" when providing their recommendations.

At the same time, the Russian team members had plenty to say about their British counterparts and their inability to say what they meant. One of the Russian team said, "On the opening call of a new project, I proposed an ambitious timeline that I believed would take months out of the implementation process. One of the British leaders replied, 'That's a brave proposal.' I thought it was a compliment and I had a green light. How was I to know that it really meant, 'That sounds overly risky, we are not on board'?"

In general, the Russians became highly frustrated with what they felt was the wishy-washy, murky communication style of their UK counterparts, which often left them confused about where they stood. As one commented, "If they would only tell us what they really mean the first time around, we could have half the number of meetings!"

In this highly complex scenario, the Russian leaders stood on one side; they were exceptionally direct in their language, very opinionated, and comfortable with conflict. On the other side were the British leaders, who were exhibiting the famed politeness and understatement associated with their country.

After meetings and conference calls, both parties would leave frustrated. Among themselves, and ultimately with HR, the Russian leaders talked about the passive-aggressive behavior of their British counterparts. They weren't saying what was really on their minds. They were saying one thing in a meeting and then another after the meeting. That undermined trust for the Russian team.

The British leaders, for their part, described the Russian team as disrespectful, rude, abrasive, inattentive, focused only on their agenda, and lacking in collaborative spirit. They ultimately shut down as well. An emotional vicious cycle got going, and the project was a mess.

This was a classic case study of what happens when you fail to read the impact you have on others. When you don't understand your audience and don't have the skills to disagree with each other in a respectful way, you lack the ability to create a win-win or to blend agendas. Ultimately, negative emotions feed on themselves, and an us vs. them attitude develops.

Many coaching sessions with the two groups were needed to bridge the communication gap, which naturally delayed the project the cohorts were collaborating on. All this is to say, advanced communications skills are necessary in the matrix from day one. Without them, you can quickly devolve into a cycle of blame and frustration, which will delay critical projects and prevent the organization from realizing the full benefits of the matrix.

## HOW TO SHARPEN YOUR COMMUNICATIONS

How do you resolve a communications issue such as the one just described between the British and Russian teams? Better yet, how can you avoid that type of breakdown altogether? There are concrete methods you can adopt that will take your communications to the advanced level you need to master for matrix success.

### Use the Right Words to Position Your Ideas

Using the right words is important. If you use too many qualifiers or hedge your perspective, you run the risk of being dismissed or perceived as underconfident. Your delivery will lack the passion and enthusiasm necessary to engender the support you want. On the other hand, if you use language that is too direct, you run the risk of appearing as though you are not collaborative.

To balance these demands, we've put together lists of phrases designed to hit the sweet spot. The key to positioning your ideas for greatest impact is to use nuanced language that persuades your audience without bullying. With that in mind, we created two collections so you are best equipped for the specific situation.

First is *invitational* language. With these phrases, you will offer your point of view clearly but will also convey an open mind. This language says to an audience, "Annie has a point of view but she doesn't have a stake in the ground. She wants to arrive at an answer together with us." These phrases are designed for the following scenarios:

- You are in the early stages of a highly collaborative project.
- You are on someone else's turf.
- You are communicating in a culture that is more indirect.

Here are some examples of invitational language:

- What if . . .
- Would it be possible . . .

- One alternative . . .
- I'd like your thoughts on . . .
- An idea I'm considering . . .
- We're leaning toward . . .
- An option I see . . .

The second collection of phrases is *convictional* language, which is most appropriate in contexts where your audience expects you to offer your opinion with assertiveness. This language will generally communicate to your stakeholders: "Sean is confident about his perspective but he's not cocky. I appreciate him giving me the best of his thinking directly, without pushing too hard." These phrases would be most useful in scenarios where:

- You are expected to be the subject matter expert.
- You are the person everyone is looking to because you have the most experience and expertise.
- You are working within a culture or an organization that you know is more direct by nature. Examples of places with more direct communication styles include Moscow, Germany, the Netherlands, and New York.

Following are examples of convictional language:

- My point of view . . .
- I recommend . . .
- I suggest . . .
- Based on our experience . . .
- My advice would be . . .
- If it were my decision, I would . . .

## Promote Healthy Debate Through Careful Language

One of the central features of a successful matrix is the exchange of diverse ideas, with the goal of arriving at the best, most informed decision. Achieving this goal depends upon debate. Not the kind of angry argument that corrodes relationships and stokes negative feelings, but the kind of dialogue in which people air opinions and raise concerns in a way that respects stakeholder voices. The process is focused on exploring ideas and finding consensus rather than on asserting a winning thesis.

This brings us to our next important skill, the ability to challenge others' ideas and engage in constructive discourse while avoiding what we call *false kindness*. If you're a person who dislikes conflict, it's easy to rationalize avoiding it. You might be saying to yourself, "I could tell Eva I disagree with her but what's the use; she's not going to listen anyway." If that's your natural orientation, then even if you do give feedback, you might use language that isn't clear enough. You might say something like, "Eva, let me tell you, I love where you're headed with this, and I think there's just tremendous upside here. I was just wondering if there was this one area we could possibly consider looking at?" Your meaning here is not clear. Although you may think you're challenging an idea, if your language isn't more candid, your point will get glossed over.

On the other hand, if your tendency is to be too direct, you can easily alienate your colleagues. Even if you're calm, expressions such as, "here's the problem with that" or "we've tried that" are enough to put people on the defensive. This is particularly true if the forum is a public one and your teammates feel as if they're being criticized. When debating an idea, measure your words and choose the right ones for the impact you want.

Whichever end of the spectrum you fall on, you will likely one day find yourself in a situation where you're called upon to speak truth to power. It's always a little daunting to tell someone with more power than you something they don't want to hear. And, yet, standing up to those with greater power is becoming an increasingly prized skill in the matrix. Remember, one of the core premises of the matrix structure is that nobody—including the most intelligent and experienced C-suite executive—will have all the information necessary to make the best decision. Top leaders are relying on the wisdom (and courage) of everyone in the organization to let them know if their thinking is incomplete.

What do you do if you feel compelled to challenge the idea of a top executive? If you deliver your message too aggressively, you run the risk of "wounding the queen or king," which can have long-term career implications. You have to know your organization and its leaders. Sometimes it's wiser to critique senior leaders' ideas one-on-one rather than in front of a group.

Below are examples of respectful but clear phrases that will enable you to challenge your team members, peers, and even your senior leadership effectively.

- An issue we may face . . .
- As we go forward, I would pay attention to . . .
- Considering the following business dynamics . . .
- In the implementation phase, I'd like us to stay focused on . . .
- A concern I have . . .
- A challenge I see . . .
- How would we respond to . . .

If you use these phrases but your stakeholder is dismissive ("I don't share your concern," "You are overthinking things," "There is always going to be risk, we need to have a bias for action"), you will have to decide whether to escalate the challenge. If you feel strongly enough to pursue the matter, choose among the following phrases, which are more direct but still land in a respectful way:

- I'm not as confident as you are . . .
- I'm not convinced this will get us where we need to be . . .

The objective is to provide clear, direct information that challenges others' thinking and leaves no question about where you stand, while simultaneously minimizing the risk of bruising egos or creating conflict.

A final point is that, while rigorous debate is essential and a sign of a healthy team, once the debate is over and the decision has been made, everyone on the team must be committed to the direction and emerge with a united front to engage the rest of the organization. If disagreement lingers after the decision has been made, the situation can quickly become toxic and devolve into a vicious cycle.

## Win-Win Problem-Solving

Now we come to a nuanced set of skills centered around constructing win-win conversations, blending agendas, and applying what we call *the soft no*. The matrix is designed to bring different perspectives to the table, but inherent in that scenario is the presence of competing agendas. This is a reality matrix leaders have to negotiate constantly.

In meetings, a stakeholder may make a request or offer a recommendation regarding the team's course, and for any number of reasons, you can't immediately commit to the suggestion. Possibly, the team lacks the bandwidth or budget to implement the idea, or perhaps it's not within policy constraints. Or you may simply feel that the request, if it was executed in that way, would not result in the best outcome for the organization. There will always be decisions/requests you disagree with. The challenge is that if you simply respond with a hard no—if you simply say, "I don't have the budget" or "I don't think that's the right way to go"—and you do that consistently, the recipient may begin to feel that the discussion routinely centers around your priorities and that you're not open to her needs. This dynamic can spiral into a toxic us vs. them scenario very quickly.

However, you can't agree to a proposal if you don't think it's in the best interests of the organization. This is where the strategies of the win-win conversation or blended agendas come in. As we break down this skill, think back to the listening skills we reviewed in chapter 4. The more you can understand the stakeholder's priorities, the better able you will be to steer the conversation in a positive direction.

When you hear a recommendation that you can't support, rather than jumping to a hard no, simply pause. Perhaps ask some open-ended questions: "Hey, I'm definitely with you on this, and I want to try to make this happen for you. It would help if I had a more complete picture. Can you tell me, again, what your main objective is? What are you hoping to achieve if we go in that direction? What would be your concern if we don't?" Listening with care shows your curiosity and your openness.

Assuming that the clarification doesn't change your thinking, you can come in with the potential pivot. Summarize your position and then offer a path by which you might arrive at a compromise. For example, you could say, "John, now that I have a more complete picture of what you're trying to achieve, I get it, and I want to help you get there. I am not able to commit to the exact proposal you have put in front of us because of some constraints. However, if we could take a step back and brainstorm, really focusing on those core objectives you're trying to achieve, I'm confident we can find a creative way to get you to your goals while still working within my budgetary constraints (or 'the bandwidth I have,' or 'the needs of the markets,' or whatever the scenario may be)." If the stakeholder has an open mind and you get into some brainstorming, your combined creativity can help you come to a solution.

We learned of a great example of a win–win approach from one of our clients in the financial services industry. Jaspreet was the learning and development leader of his company's Asia Pacific region. The global head of L&D had put forth a strategy to drive more content consistency in their leadership development programs globally. Historically, the company's regions had a great deal of autonomy in selecting and designing their training, often working with a variety of local consulting and training companies. A core driver of the new strategy was to leverage global best-in-class training content to ensure that employees around the world were benefitting from the same content. Another goal of the initiative was to reduce the cost from the use of external vendors and suppliers. The objective was to move training programs internally, where business leaders would become certified and trained as facilitators of the content.

When Jaspreet met with Deepa, his field L&D leader who supported India (one of the largest and most profitable markets), to present this strategy and gain her support, he encountered some clear points of resistance. First, Deepa explained her concern that the training was not developed in their region and thus would be suboptimal for her people. Particularly, she felt the content taken from other parts of the world would lack the cultural understanding and nuance needed for her group. Additionally, she shared that there were long-established relationships with certain training companies and consultants that the India leadership team was very confident in, and the decision to no longer engage these training consultants would cause a lot of tension. For these reasons, Deepa did not feel she could support this new initiative, even though she agreed with the high-level goals of greater content consistency and reduced costs.

Jaspreet listened carefully and communicated his understanding. He shared that he understood from his own experience the power of long-standing relationships with trusted training partners. He also made it clear that he understood how important it was that she maintain positive relationships and credibility with the country's leadership team. Next, he invited Deepa into a win-win conversation and proposed the following ideas:

- What if Deepa and her L&D team had the opportunity to review all of the training content selected as best-in-class globally, and had the flexibility to make whatever additions, enhancements, and changes they felt necessary to ensure it was customized to their region's culture, as long as the core learning remained intact?
- What if the training company she had a long-standing relationship with was hired to train the internal business leaders in the new content? This would not only continue the relationship, but since the leadership team had confidence in their teaching approach and facilitation style, this would help to develop quality internal trainers. This plan would lead to a substantial reduction in the amount of work the training company facilitated over time, but the decline would be more gradual.
- What if the training company continued to facilitate the high-touch leadership sessions, where their unique expertise and credibility were essential for success?

After some additional discussion, Deepa felt she could sign on to this approach. In this classic win-win, Jaspreet achieved the primary goals of the new global L&D strategy—driving content consistency, developing internal trainers to deliver materials, and reducing the amount spent on external vendors—and Deepa met her primary needs to ensure the content was culturally aligned, that a positive relationship with the outside training company would remain, and that the senior leadership would not feel like the quality of their training would be diminished. At the end of the conversation, both felt that this approach would put Deepa and her team in a position to successfully drive this change initiative.

Here are some phrases to begin a win-win conversation:

- "I couldn't commit to doing it exactly the way you are suggesting, but I want to try my best to meet your needs. Are you open to brainstorming some alternative ways we can meet your needs?"
- "Given the projects we are currently committed to . . ."
- "Given the constraints of our resources and people . . ."

## Blending Agendas

Blending agendas is another communication strategy designed to create a win-win. In this scenario, you find yourself having a dialog with a stakeholder who is focused on achieving $X$ while you really want to achieve $Y$. Sometimes, the smart approach is to say, "I'm willing to let go of 30 percent of what I'm trying to achieve because it's more important that 70 percent happens than nothing at all."

We observed excellent work blending agendas while consulting with a global restaurant company. The scenario unfolded as this organization's global marketing center of excellence (COE) identified that consistent international brand messaging would provide more efficiency and better brand management. Historically, this organization's regional and country leaders had considerable flexibility in developing campaigns they felt were most effective with their local customers. As a result, the variation in brand messaging across the globe was vast.

Once this new global strategy of brand consistency was decided, Francisca, VP of global marketing and lead of the global marketing COE, went to a number of meetings with her regional and country marketing counterparts to share the new direction. Fortunately, Francisca employed many of the influencing and collaboration skills we have shared in the book. She quickly picked up on the fact that many of the regional and country marketing stakeholders were hesitant about this approach. As she continued to ask deeper questions and gain understanding, it became clear that, while the local marketing teams were open to some of the core brand messages the COE wanted to roll out, they felt the campaign was missing certain niche elements that were extremely important to their consumers.

Knowing how important the enthusiastic support of regional marketing leaders was to the success of this initiative, Francisca proposed an integrated solution. If the regional marketing team would commit to aligning with the core brand messages the global team was focused on, they could retain the flexibility to add some marketing campaigns that addressed the unique aspects of their consumer base. This way, both teams got what they cared about most and found a way to collaborate. The outcome was not 100 percent global uniformity, as Francisca had originally proposed; however, based on her skillful compromise, she achieved 80 percent of her objective while solidifying a powerful partnership with her field marketing leaders.

## Using the Soft No

In one scenario common in the matrix, a stakeholder requests help, time, or resources that you simply do not have available because of other priorities. In these circumstances, a soft no could be the way to go.

Here is an example that involves an R&D group we worked with. Historically, pre-matrix, the R&D team would not only make recommendations about how to inaugurate a new product or idea, they would be on the ground at the plants or facilities to run the installation. So the organization got used to that. In the matrix, a pivot was underway. Now the R&D group was more focused at a strategic level rather than on implementation. But when that transition first occurred, the plants were not happy because they had an expectation that the old on-site assistance would continue. Quite a few individuals on the R&D and operations teams were not skillful in the way they handled the transition. When plant managers called them, they gave the factually correct answer, which was "Sorry, we no longer do that. That's not our role. We've been asked to focus on a more strategic level so I can't help you with that." All true. But the message wasn't delivered in the right way. By the time we began working with the R&D team, they had become known as the "No" group. This is not an ideal perception for others in your organization to have in any scenario, but it's especially damaging when you are trying to engender collaborative relationships.

To help the R&D team shift this negative perception and improve stakeholder relationships, we coached the teams in how to deliver a soft no. The soft no says, "I'm not going to agree to what I shouldn't, but I'm going to demonstrate my willingness to help and try to be supportive." In the scenario with the R&D team, they decided on the following approach: R&D gets a call from the plant, saying they've got this new idea and are wondering when the R&D team can come for the installation. Instead of replying, "That's no longer our department," R&D was coached to respond with a soft no: "I appreciate you reaching out. There has been a transition here, so with the org changes and our new focus, we no longer have the bandwidth to do the implementation ourselves. However, because I know this is a change and I want to support you and make this as seamless as possible, here are some options I hope will be helpful for these next couple of implementations. One option is that you send a few of the folks from your plant up to spend a few hours with me and my team, and we can give them specific instructions, share best practices, and let them know processes that have worked well for us in the past. Or, if some of your team wants to come by and have lunch and talk through implementation strategy, we could do that as well. Finally, here's the name of a consultant we've used who can work with you."

The point of the response is to make sincere gestures and offers of help without resorting to either the *hard no*, which is upsetting to the receiver, or continuing to agree when you don't have the resources to do it. Ideally, of course, people prefer to hear yes, but the soft no signals that you are collaborative, and that you want to help but there are limits to what you can do. Almost anyone can live with a soft no.

Below are additional soft-no strategies you can draw on if your stakeholders are asking you to commit time or resources you do not currently have available:

- "Could we do this later in the year?"
- "Perhaps I could be a part of a meeting and give you the best of my thinking on how one of your people could take the lead?"
- "Perhaps I could act as an advisor to one of your people?"
- "I know some external consultants that may be able to help with this."

If you cannot find a win-win solution and your soft-no approach is not accepted by this stakeholder despite your best efforts to find an alternative, use one of these phrases:

- "It's not my call to shift our priorities, but I can take this back to [our group leader], and if he tells me we can shift the priorities, I would be happy to help."
- "I appreciate your willingness to explore a win-win solution, but it looks like we haven't been able to come up with one yet. Let me take this back to [our group leader], and perhaps she can think of a better alternative."

## THE LIMBIC SYSTEM

We've talked about the importance of mastering advanced communication skills, and about how subtle and nuanced your communication must be. You need to be on your game to harness your talents in this arena, and that is hard enough to do when you're calm, poised, and mindful.

Imagine how difficult effective communication can be if you lose your cool. If you find yourself in a circumstance where emotions take over, you might communicate in ways that can damage your relationships and impact trust for the long term. Unfortunately, you need to display only a few of these lapses—especially in a highly collaborative, integrated matrix—to create a negative perception.

## Our Caveman Brains

Because unfettered emotional outbursts can be so dangerous to the matrix, let's spend a little time looking at the limbic system, a part of the brain that controls basic emotions and drives. We won't get too deep into the neuroscience, but here are the essentials: Different parts of our brains govern our behavior. The frontal lobe, located just behind the forehead, is by far the most evolutionarily advanced part of the human brain. It is associated with executive function and is often referred to as the CEO of the brain because of its logical orientation and rational calm.

We have another set of brain structures, called the limbic system, which is part of the overall autonomic nervous system. It is nicknamed the *caveman brain* because it houses the fight-or-flight impulse that, from an evolutionary standpoint, has been around for a lot longer than our forebrain. That's for good reason. Historically, many scenarios required that we humans make life-or-death decisions in an instant; for example, if a saber-toothed tiger jumped out from the grass. We needed the limbic system to kick in and help us survive the attack without wasting precious time. When the limbic system is triggered, you react without thinking because you're fighting or fleeing for your life.

The problem, of course, is that many types of perceived threats can trigger a limbic-system response, and that adrenaline-fueled behavior wreaks havoc on our intentions when it comes to communicating in a global business environment. Think about road rage and rush-hour traffic. Research shows that up to 60 percent of Americans admit that if they're driving down the highway and somebody suddenly cuts them off, they will retaliate with unsafe driving maneuvers, threaten the other driver, or resort to rude gestures. Sometimes these responses lead to tragedies that appear in the news as car accidents or heart attacks. The point is, when we hear those stories, our first reaction is: "What were they thinking?" But when the limbic system takes over, we no longer *are* thinking—or at least we're not thinking rationally.

The important information to know for matrix collaboration is that, if our buttons get pushed and we go limbic, our listening skills essentially go out the window. We tend to interrupt, our speech patterns change, and the register of our voices goes up. We also tend to use exaggerated language, and responses can get worse from there. We may:

- use accusatory language ("This always happens . . . ," "You never . . . ," "Every time . . .")
- curse/name call (use labels)
- yell
- order/direct ("You have to . . . ," "You must . . .")
- use threatening language ("You have no idea who you are dealing with . . .")

To avoid explosive encounters, which can damage relationships permanently, everyone in global business today should have a strategy for dealing with the limbic system—yours and others'.

We all know people whose limbic systems take over on a rather frequent basis, while others are much calmer in their orientation and are impacted by their limbic reactions far less often. But we're all human beings, and we are all susceptible to emotional responses.

## Managing the Limbic System

Make sure you have a healthy respect for your limbic system. It is powerful and primitive, and when it takes over, it can cause a lot of damage in a very short period of time. Here are some tips and tools for managing the limbic system:

- **Cultivate self-awareness.** Do you know what pushes your buttons? Is it somebody who throws others under the bus, takes credit, or assigns blame? Perhaps you are triggered by a person who is disrespectful or rude, or who talks to people like he is better than they are? Your personal peeves could encompass any number of discourteous acts. The key is to understand which behaviors can prompt a limbic system response very quickly. Over time, certain individuals can themselves become our limbic triggers: all they have to do is walk into a room and our limbic systems jump into action.

- **Be attuned to early signals from your body.** The limbic system stimulates a physiological reaction. When you find yourself gritting your teeth, fidgeting, or feeling heat rise in your body, pick up on your response and catch yourself before you say something ill-advised. That's a win. Even though you may have felt angry, you prevented yourself from doing any long-term damage, which is our main objective here.
- **Know that, while the limbic system can activate at any moment, it's more likely if you are overtired, overworked, stressed, overly busy, or immunocompromised.** No matter who you are, the fuse that sets off your limbic system is much, much shorter when you are under some form of stress.

A few strategies for managing the limbic system are specific to the global workplace. For example, everyone today needs a limbic email strategy. If you receive an email that pushes your buttons, step away from the computer. Go for a walk. Take some deep breaths. If delaying your response is an option, draft the email the next day when you are calmer.

There's also a strategy we call the cathartic email. Write your response in a word-processing document. You can say whatever you want, but don't place the text anywhere near an email address and a send button. You never want to be in a situation where a twitch of the finger ends in disaster.

Conference calls are another venue that demands an emotion-diffusing strategy. Obviously, you have the benefit of the mute button. If someone on the call says something that sets you off, mute yourself and count to five to collect yourself before responding. Remember that, if you are on a conference call in an office and others are in the room, they are seeing your reaction. Even though the other party on the call doesn't see you, you must do your best to manage your limbic reaction for those who share the room with you at that moment.

In a person-to-person situation, if you find yourself starting to react poorly, consider excusing yourself for a moment. Grab your cell phone and claim an emergency, or simply tell the other person that you have to step out briefly. Let yourself breathe. Calm down. Come back when you're in a better place. Generally, you should not communicate when your limbic system is on the edge of control; you will only inject negativity into the situation.

Some of these strategies may seem awkward at first, but know that we've field-tested and proven them over time in matrix organizations. If you feel clumsy initially, that's okay. As with any new skill, the more you practice, the more natural your communication will become.

---

## YOUR MATRIX MOMENT: HONING ADVANCED COMMUNICATION SKILLS

- Consider cultural differences that affect the way people communicate, and work to bridge communication gaps created by direct and indirect language styles.
- To communicate at the advanced level required in the matrix:
  - position your ideas so they have optimal impact by using invitational or convictional language
  - promote healthy debate
  - search for win-win solutions
  - blend agendas when working with multiple stakeholders

Be mindful of your limbic system. Don't allow an emotional fight-or-flight response to dictate the way you communicate and interact with others. Learn to recognize when your limbic system becomes activated and manage those emotions to prevent outbursts that could damage relationships.

## CREATING YOUR ADVANCED COMMUNICATION ACTION PLAN

In this chapter, we covered several scenarios in which advanced communication skills are essential. Now it's time to create your communication action plan. Take a minute to think about the important meetings you have scheduled. Can any of the scenarios discussed in this chapter help you better communicate your ideas while successfully navigating relationships among stakeholders? Use the following questions to identify areas needing improvement and to form your plan to address them:

- **Positioning your ideas.** Do you have an upcoming meeting where you will have to offer your ideas? What language do you plan to use? Will it be invitational or convictional?
- **Preparing for a healthy debate.** Do you foresee having to challenge others in upcoming meetings? What language will you use to encourage a healthy debate and to keep the exchange respectful?
- **Finding the win-win.** Is there an impending situation where you will have to find a win-win solution? What language can you use to jump-start those conversations?
- **Blending agendas.** If you are facing a scenario that requires you to blend multiple agendas, what strategy do you plan to use to achieve your desired outcome?
- **Using the soft no.** Is there an upcoming scenario where you may need to use a soft no? What phrasing do you plan to use?
- **Managing your limbic system.** What strategies will you use in the event your limbic system is triggered during an exchange? Have you had to manage your fight-or-flight reactions in the past? Think back to what worked and what didn't. What is your plan moving forward?

# A FINAL WORD ON ADVANCED
# COMMUNICATIONS

Communicating and collaborating effectively in a matrix are skills that are consistently underestimated by leaders who are used to engaging and inspiring the people they work with. You may think you have mastered this area, but in a matrix you need *advanced* communication skills. In this chapter, we've surveyed the next-level skills and tools you need to communicate effectively across your organization by positioning your ideas effectively, facilitating healthy debate, finding the win-win, blending agendas, and deploying the soft no. In employing these practices and learning to manage your limbic reactions during stressful situations, you can bring a steady voice to collaborative efforts, ensuring that your team arrives at the superior, innovative solutions the matrix promises.

CHAPTER 7

❖

# Elevating Your Impact
# in Meetings

EVERYONE LOVES TO HATE MEETINGS. A constant in organizational life, meetings are so ubiquitous that we treat them like the weather: sometimes good, sometimes bad, always running in the background of our daily lives. Occasionally, meetings are engaging, but most of the time we simply endure them. We check our phones. We doodle on our legal pads. We wait for the meeting to be over so we can get back to our *real* work. Taking meetings for granted is a common matrix pitfall, however. In a highly collaborative environment, a meeting isn't an ordinary office interaction, it is the main stage.

We have seen many leaders put hours, days, or weeks into a project but fail to prepare themselves to perform optimally at the meeting. They are committed to their work but don't know how to maximize their impact when they present their ideas. In a matrix world, the most consequential decisions are shaped or made in meetings. These may be traditional in-person gatherings, technology-facilitated meetings at which the participants are visible to each other but not in the same location, or even ordinary conference calls. Meetings are where it all happens.

Success at a matrix meeting is critical. Because the stakeholders often come from different parts of the business, and even different geographic locations, if you are not able to make the most of the meeting time, you could be missing a critical opportunity. This isn't always true in a traditional, hierarchical company. In that setting, meetings are mainly oriented "vertically": they involve members of the same localized work group, ranging from senior to lower-ranking members. If you feel as though you missed the mark in a meeting (i.e., you didn't get the chance to make your point or felt like your delivery was a little off), it's likely you can walk down the hall after the meeting and tell the relevant stakeholders what you wanted them to know. No big deal.

In the matrix, you may not have that option. The meetings you attend will not always be vertical; they may be horizontal, featuring stakeholders from across business groups, functions, and time zones. These are not individuals you can easily find later at the watercooler for a supplemental chat. The meeting may be your best, or indeed your only, chance to command their attention. Each of these meetings has the potential to determine the direction this matrix group takes, so you must make them count. Meetings are where collaboration takes place, where innovation happens, where ideas are exchanged. While a certain amount of influencing clearly happens behind the scenes—before and after the meeting—the matrix, more than any other organizational structure, is driven by the outcome of meetings.

Yet, even with so much at stake, we regularly observe smart, hardworking, and dedicated leaders who fail to place a high enough priority on preparing for key meetings. This is understandable given how busy leaders are, but that doesn't mean it's wise. The most successful matrix leaders are the ones who can effectively leverage meeting time to:

- drive their ideas forward
- command the respect of their stakeholders
- ensure their voices are heard

The leaders who can achieve these objectives most consistently will have the greatest positive impact on their organizations while demonstrating that they have the executive presence, gravitas, and influencing ability to lead their companies into the future. They are the stars of the matrix organization, and it's their prowess in ordinary, everyday meetings that grants them such power. All this is to say that elevating your impact in meetings is not optional for the matrix leader; it's required.

So, let's break down the steps and look closely at what it takes to achieve matrix meeting success.

As a matrix leader, you need to focus on three essential areas to ensure you are maximizing your impact in meetings. First is the *pre-meeting preparation* that ensures you have done adequate reflection and developed the right game plan heading into the meeting. Your strategy must be geared toward the specific agenda and stakeholders. Second is *effectiveness*. In meetings, you must employ a range of intentional insights, skills, and strategies to help you demonstrate the executive presence that will bolster your credibility and level of influence. *Post-meeting activities are the third essential.* Whether this is following up with people, doing what you said you would do, or researching to learn more about the subject, your impact doesn't end when the meeting ends.

In this chapter, we will break down these areas in great detail. Rather than presenting a purely conceptual discussion of these important skill areas, we will provide you with a step-by-step process that you can easily incorporate into your professional life, beginning tomorrow. This is where many of the skills and insights you have learned in previous chapters come into play.

## PRE-MEETING PREPARATION

Considering the well-established dynamics and myriad factors involved when collaborating with and influencing your stakeholders, it is generally unwise to show up to critical meetings without doing some deliberate analysis and developing a strategic approach. To put it frankly, you have to do your homework. Going into a meeting "cold"—particularly with all the information swirling in your brain from the other meetings and interactions you have in a day—and trusting that you will spontaneously engage in an optimal way is a gamble. And with so much at stake, it is not a gamble we recommend. In fact, one of the attributes of the busy world we live in is "cognitive overload," a condition in which our brains are overwhelmed by so much information that we can't think clearly. Even if you are naturally comfortable in a group setting, your approach and strategy won't be well organized and coordinated unless you devote time to preparation.

For the most consequential meetings, we urge you to reflect on the following areas in advance:

1. AGENDA
   - **Based on the agenda, what is my plan to impact the discussion?** By studying the agenda in advance and identifying key areas where you have value to add, you can go into the meeting more relaxed and without the pressure to spontaneously come up with brilliant input.
   - **Is there an opportunity to bring a more strategic perspective into the discussion?** Elevating the discussion and offering a disruptive, strategic idea is good for you and, generally, the team. However, this is more difficult to arrive at spontaneously, so allow yourself plenty of advance thinking time; the likelihood that you will spot a strategic opportunity and articulate it cogently skyrockets when you have done some groundwork.

2. STAKEHOLDERS
   - **What do I know about the stakeholders' agendas and priorities in advance of the meeting?** How can I factor that information into my discussion? What questions can I ask to deepen my understanding? This is the time to lean on your influencing skills and utilize the various avenues available to discover this important information, both in advance of and during the meeting, then shape the focus of your ideas accordingly.
   - **Which network connections should I check in with to gather information or build alignment in advance?** (See chapter 3.)
   - **Are there any particular points of resistance I should anticipate?** (See chapter 4.)

- **What do I know about the power dynamics that I should remain mindful of?** (See chapter 5.)

3. EXECUTIVE VOCABULARY
   (THIS IS WHERE CHAPTER 6 WILL BE HELPFUL.)
   - **What language will I use to maximize my impact?**
   - **What phrases will I use to stimulate healthy debate, if needed?**
   - **Am I prepared for a possible win-win or soft-no discussion, if the occasion arises?**

As you work through your pre-meeting preparation and reflection questions, several outcomes are likely. First, you will dramatically increase the odds that you have considered much (if not all) of the essential information you need to develop a thoughtful approach. Next, by putting this reflection on paper (or in a computer document), you are creating both a strategic approach and a kind of script that will ensure your communication is on point. Once you have your reflection and plan in place, you have the luxury of simply reviewing it the day of the meeting to guarantee your thoughts are well organized.

Is there a possibility that one of your stakeholders may take the discussion on a tangent or veer off the original agenda? Sure. Anything is possible. While you need to have a plan, you do not want to be overly rigid. Flexibility and agility are important (this is why the skill of reading stakeholder tells is so valuable). While an off-the-cuff, intuitive approach to meeting participation may work occasionally, we will bet on the well-prepared leader every time.

Another possible outcome, as you reflect on these questions, may be unpleasant in the near term but can represent an important call to action. This scenario is that you draw a blank on many of the pre-meeting questions. To address this unhappy chance, we recommend that you do your pre-meeting exercise a minimum of forty-eight hours before the scheduled meeting. This gives you some time to close your information gap, if necessary, so you can contribute in a meaningful way.

## EFFECTIVENESS IN MEETINGS

Now that you've done your homework and are ready for the big meeting, let's turn our focus to the way you show up and perform in the meeting. You have the information you need and you have a plan—now you must execute it.

*Executive presence*, a buzzword in global business, is one of the qualities that organizations most prize in their leaders. Considering the premium placed on a leader's ability to inspire, lead with passion, persuade, and develop followership, it is easy to see why this ability to demonstrate gravitas and command a room is viewed as a key differentiator.

Like strategic thinking, executive presence is sometimes seen as purely personality driven, a quality that a leader either possesses or does not, rather than a skill that can be learned. You have probably heard the assertion, "You've either got it or you don't." Understandably, many leaders are discouraged when given feedback such as, "increase your leadership presence," thinking to themselves, "I have never been the world's most charismatic person . . . I guess I am limited in my career." In fact, when we ask leaders to describe executive presence, many say things like, "It's the 'it' factor. It's hard to describe, but I know it when I see it." This is not exactly actionable feedback. In the next section, we break down the ways you can enhance your effectiveness in meetings and display the executive presence that stakeholders look for. Anyone can enhance her executive presence if she is willing to make the effort. The good news is that if you *don't* have it, you can get it!

### Cultivating Confidence

We've interviewed thousands of senior leaders, and we often ask them to describe the qualities and behaviors that convey executive presence to them. Near the top of virtually everyone's list is confidence. When people who have executive presence speak, they project a self-assurance that engenders a high level of credibility. We all begin on different points of the spectrum with regard to our confidence in presenting to groups or participating in meetings. Naturally, where you fall on this continuum will determine how you prioritize cultivating confidence. Additionally, your confidence level in any particular situation is likely to be based on how familiar you are with the audience, how comfortable you are with the subject matter, the level of seniority in the room, and what is at stake. Regardless of circumstance, the confidence you project is the foundation of your stakeholders' trust. The question, then, is, "How can I ensure that I am showing up in a way that is perceived as confident, and that feels authentic rather than contrived?"

Fortunately, the latest research in neuroscience and positive psychology has shown that a number of techniques can help access our natural feelings of confidence. Take a few minutes and try these two exercises:

1. **Focus on your strengths.** On a sheet of paper, write two or three of your greatest strengths as a professional. Perhaps you're exceptional at coaching and mentoring, or maybe you excel at problem-solving. Once you have listed them, think of a time when these strengths led to a positive impact on your colleagues or the business. Soak in your successes and see what happens. You will feel more confident in a matter of minutes.
2. **Reflect on your advocates.** Another powerful exercise is to think of people who believe in your talent and potential, both in the past and currently. These are the people who have invested in you, who have shared why they believe in you. Triggering those memories can help you find a more confident place.

## Appropriate Participation

It is difficult to convey a sense of executive presence and influence those in the meeting if you underparticipate or wait to get into the conversation. As obvious as this statement is, we see underparticipation with extraordinary frequency. At the same time, if you dominate the conversation, interrupt others, or ramble on, you can leave an equally negative impression on stakeholders. Finding the sweet spot of appropriate participation is critical.

The best gauge of whether you are under- or overparticipating involves reflecting on your own performance and gathering some feedback. There are typically two main personality characteristics at play when people do not contribute appropriately at meetings: 1) the need for attention and 2) the need for certainty.

If you are comfortable with a microphone in your hand, often find yourself the life of the party (or meeting), and tend to seek attention, you are probably not underparticipating. An outgoing personality can give you a natural advantage in a world where so much happens in meetings, because you are in your comfort zone in a social setting. That said, check in about whether you are potentially overplaying your strength. Are you focusing enough on listening to others? Are you sincerely valuing the perspectives of others, considering them, and building upon them? Or, are you primarily waiting for an opening to share your brilliant point of view? If you find yourself unsure, ask for some feedback from trusted colleagues.

The other personality driver to consider with regard to overparticipation is a need for certainty. This refers to the degree to which you value precision and accuracy, and to which you feel the need to work hard to avoid mistakes. If your need for certainty is on the lower end of the continuum, you are likely more intuitive and spontaneous; you feel comfortable shooting from the hip without analyzing your idea first, and you have an inherent ease with brainstorming. Leverage that advantage, but keep in mind that if you are too quick to let your opinions fly, you may lose credibility or begin to dominate.

If any of these descriptions resonated with you—or you have been given feedback that they should—the useful self-talk below can help you find your participation comfort zone:

- "What do these people know that I don't?"
- "To collaborate effectively, my stakeholders need to feel heard."
- "Remember to listen first and build on others' ideas when possible."

The opposite scenario, in which a person underparticipates or gets into the discussion too late, is more common and perhaps more damaging. The research is clear: If you are attending meetings and staying quiet, senior leaders and stakeholders are not thinking, "I really appreciate John's deeply reflective nature and modesty." More likely, they are thinking, "John is not a thought leader, he does not lead from the front." If you have an inherently low need for attention, prefer one-on-one meetings or smaller groups, and notice that in larger and unfamiliar groups you get quiet, then you may be vulnerable to underparticipation. Similarly, if you have a high need for certainty and like to take your time to think about the best answer or are concerned about being wrong, you may be entering conversations too late to have an impact. If any of these descriptors resonate, use the self-talk below to build "decent boldness" and participate frequently enough and early enough in the meeting:

- "I can't lose what I don't have."
- "The real risk is saying nothing at all and leaving an impression that I lack confidence and do not add value."
- "I got this far in my career by being confident in myself and coming through under pressure."
- "I have important information and can add immense value to the meeting."
- "I've done my homework and am confident in my data and knowledge in this matter."
- "This is a great opportunity for me to showcase my expertise and talent."

## Communication Agility

Another top behavior that drives effectiveness in meetings and demonstrates executive presence is a leader's ability to "read the room" and adjust in the moment. This is what we call *communication agility*. Fortunately, you already have the preparation covered, so you can feel confident in your depth of content knowledge and your approach. As a result, you don't have to read every slide during your PowerPoint presentation out of fear you might miss something. Rather, you keep your focus on the audience and are able to pivot to meet them where they are. This is an impressive ability that will set you apart in the minds of senior leaders as well as elevate your capacity to influence and persuade. Communication agility builds on a skill we introduced in previous chapters: reading stakeholder tells. You already know how to apply this technique to discover and react to stakeholder priorities, resistance, and power dynamics. Following are some additional tips for reading tells to help you better engage your stakeholders in meetings:

*Impatience*

> *What to look for:* You're giving a presentation or sharing your ideas, and some of the more senior people in the room are looking ahead in the presentation, fidgeting, or getting on their mobile devices. They're no longer listening because they're frustrated by your pace.

> *What to do:* Obviously, you don't want to point out that you're noticing their impatience. But you could pause and say, "I realize how precious everyone's time is, so let me just boil it down to the key points. From there, I'd love to get some guidance from you. Where would you like me to focus the discussion?"

*The Group Is "Sold"*

> *What to look for:* This sounds like a good problem to have. You shared your strategy so effectively that your audience is on board. However, you continue with your persuasion efforts because that's what you'd planned, even though the critical stakeholders are already convinced. This can cause considerable frustration. You will notice a change in the behavior of stakeholders who have been giving you signals of interest for a while; they've been tracking your presentation with great interest and nodding their heads clearly. Then, they start to display signs of impatience.

> *What to do:* If you see and feel that you have achieved your goal and have obtained buy-in from the key stakeholders, move on to other points or wrap up the meeting early. There is no need to continue

trying to "sell" them if they are already sold. Say something like, "It looks to me like you are all on board with the plan, which is really exciting. To be efficient with the rest of our time, are there any other points/items you would like me to focus on? Do you have any questions?"

## Confusion

*What to look for:* You're offering your perspective on a point, and you notice eyes start to glaze over a little. Maybe there's some brow furrowing. A number of stakeholders do not seem to be tracking your line of reasoning. You may see people looking at each other in confusion.

*What to do:* Remember that in the matrix, people attending may be from different functions or different parts of the business, and they may not have the expertise or knowledge about a certain subject that you have. If you pick up cues that some attendees are not following your line of thought or may be confused, you don't want to embarrass them or put them on the spot. Instead, take a natural pause and say, "I recognize that I talk about these things every day. This is all very familiar to me but I imagine some of you may be hearing about it for the first time. So I want to pause here and see what questions you have and what I may be able to clarify." This is a moment where you can quickly catch any audience members who may potentially be drifting and bring them right back into the fold.

## Effective Communication

The way you communicate in meetings will have a dramatic impact on whether you are seen as possessing executive presence. Based on the latest research in leadership development and our own experience as executive coaches, a number of subtle signs are associated with this all-important characteristic. The communication nuances most looked for in a leader are:

- crisp and focused messaging
- a bias for action
- confidence in communicating, while avoiding arrogance
- the courage to challenge others (in a respectful manner)
- the ability to deal with conflict
- the capacity to lead from the front

One of the benefits of preparing, planning, and rehearsing for meetings is that you will be crisper and more focused in your delivery because you are not thinking of explanations or rationales on the spot. We advocate the "What, So What, Now What" approach to keeping discussion focused. This technique of preparation and delivery involves clearly outlining *what* you are there to discuss, the opportunity (or challenge) that is before you. Immediately pivot and lay out reasons they should care, answering the question, *So what?* Why is this opportunity/challenge critical to the group of stakeholders listening? Why should they prioritize pursuing or solving it? Finally, shift focus and address: *Now what?* What concrete actions do you recommend in order to achieve the desired outcome? This approach will keep you focused and avoids the risk of a meandering discussion that can quickly frustrate stakeholders.

Another advantage of taking the time to prepare is that you can plan the language you will use and muster the confidence you want to project. Your executive vocabulary will serve you well here. Anticipating your audience's reaction increases the odds that you will be ready for the constructive discourse that is likely to follow; you can have at hand proven phrases that allow you to challenge others without offending them or coming across as arrogant.

Don't underestimate the importance of engaging in the discussion early. If you wait until most of the others have shared opinions before giving your point of view, you may be seen as tentative or lacking confidence. Certainly, you will not be viewed as leading from the front, a quality that is generally preferred.

A final point on communication in meetings concerns the admiration given to leaders who demonstrate a bias for action. This doesn't mean forcing a conversation or jamming a solution down the group's throat. However, when the discussion has been robust and everyone has been heard, stepping up to take the lead on the next moves can cast a positive light on you and create the perception that you are a person who gets things done.

## Advantageous Seating

The need to protect your seat at the table is commonly overlooked in discussions of meeting effectiveness and executive presence. But it can be as important as any other factor. This skill begins with finding your best physical seat at the table, which sets you up for success at the start of the meeting. If you take a seat toward the back or side of the room, you risk sending the signal that you lack confidence or are disengaged. Choose your seat wisely. Think, for example, about sitting at a corner of the table, so that you can see everyone and your perspective is wide and open. Or consider a seat close to the more senior leader(s) in the room, communicating that you know where you belong. Seat choice is an important nonverbal signal. Don't overlook it.

As you work to capitalize on your time at meetings, focus on protecting your status, your figurative "seat at the table." This is particularly important if you work within an organization where many of the stakeholders are comfortable speaking and are quite assertive and fast-paced in their delivery. If you wait for someone to pause and ask you for your opinion, you might well sit there the entire meeting and never get a word in. Several scenarios can be tricky to navigate, and you must be prepared to handle them when they arise:

- Someone interrupts you midsentence.
- The group simply talks over one another and doesn't make space for you in the discussion.
- A colleague moves the focus away from your key topic before the discussion has concluded.
- Someone takes up time that was allotted to you on the agenda.

Responding fruitfully in these scenarios is a balancing act. If you react in a way that is emotionally abrupt, you may create conflict and appear impatient or boorish. On the other hand, if you are firm and clear, and establish your presence in the room, you can dramatically intensify your impact. Below are a number of phrases you can use to assert yourself without overreacting:

- "Before we move on, I'd like some feedback or a reaction to the point I just made."
- "In order to bring completion to this topic, I want to finish my suggestion."
- "I'd like to jump in here . . ."
- "To build on that point . . ."

## POST-MEETING ACTIVITIES

The meeting is over; now what? We've coached many leaders who, after meetings are over, think to themselves, "Thank goodness that's over. Now I can get back to my work." That's a big mistake. Once the meeting breaks, you aren't finished: it's on to the post-meeting checklist. Spend just ten to fifteen minutes on the following actions right after a meeting:

- **Follow up on any outstanding items.** Are there elements of your agenda that were not addressed? Did you agree to any actions in the meeting? It is critical that you take stock of these and be sure to execute them efficiently and within the time period you promised. Don't let follow-ups wait. Build on the momentum of the meeting to carry out post-meeting actions.
- **Circle back with your network.** No matter how you thought you performed in the meeting, connect with members of your network to get their opinions on how it went. You may have missed some details or reactions. If you can reach out to someone who was in the meeting, great! If not, contact people in your network who are in a position to hear from someone who attended the meeting.

- **Address any issues that came up.** One important element of meetings in the matrix is the issue of being "heard." Obviously, if an individual spoke in a meeting, the other attendees perceived their words. But did everyone "hear" them? That is, did the meeting members take what was said seriously? You can answer that question by taking action to address any issues that came up in the meeting.

## CASE STUDY: MISSED OPPORTUNITIES

Natalie is a high-potential marketing leader for a global consumer products company. During the early stages of her career, Natalie stood out because of her powerful combination of creative marketing skills and analytical depth. She was known for her ability to delve into the numbers and quickly identify patterns, then formulate innovative solutions. And, she had an intuitive sense that allowed her to create these successful solutions with very little guidance. Her managers often praised her autonomous and independent nature: "You just have to task Natalie with a challenge or objective and she is off running. And more often than not she will come back with an excellent solution and outcome."

She moved up rapidly from analyst to senior manager. After considering Natalie's strong track record and ability, headquarters decided to promote her to senior director of one of the company's biggest divisions, and she was put in charge of two of the division's major brands. Natalie now sat on the division's senior leader team (SLT), which was made up of more experienced and senior leaders.

Understandably, Natalie was hesitant to share her ideas in the SLT meetings, even though she often had opinions. This leadership team was composed of experienced and talented leaders who had their fair share of confidence and strong opinions, and they were not shy about voicing them. In this group, if you were not proactive and assertive about getting your ideas on the table, the meeting would come and go quickly without your contribution. As a result, Natalie's participation was consistently on the lower end of frequency.

In addition to Natalie's predictable hesitation in offering her opinions at meetings, she didn't feel the need to talk "just to hear myself talk." Her perspective was that, unless her point was mission critical, she wouldn't communicate it; if she did have an opinion, she preferred to take it "off-line" with one or two stakeholders to make meetings more efficient. In her previous roles, most of the critical interactions she had with senior leaders were in one-on-one discussions. Ultimately, she had always been rewarded for her outstanding innovation, work product, and results, so standing out in meetings had never been a priority for her. Unless she was a formal presenter, she did not prepare for meetings but rather showed up with an open mind and then observed how things unfolded.

Natalie went about her new role as she had in the past, digging deeply into the challenges of the brands she had been newly assigned to and working with her team to develop innovative solutions. When Natalie shared her ideas with the division president, Jane was very supportive of the ideas and encouraged Natalie to move forward with them. Natalie also spent plenty of time in one-on-one meetings with her peers to brainstorm, share ideas, and align. However, in the SLT meetings she tended to do more listening than talking.

After several months, Jane asked Natalie to come into her office to discuss her transition into the new role. She gave Natalie high praise for how quickly she had grasped the brands and their challenges, and the great creative solutions she was putting into action. However, she expressed concern over what she observed as Natalie's underparticipation and lack of impact in meetings. She cited the lack of frequency with which Natalie weighed in on discussions, and said she was particularly struck by this because she knew how many great ideas Natalie had when they held their one-on-one meetings. She explained to Natalie, "As a leader on our team, you are expected to influence the team's thinking beyond just your brands and even the marketing function. The other stakeholders who are part of the SLT count on your input and thought leadership—this is why our team is so integrated."

In addition, she shared that she had received feedback from other SLT members that Natalie possibly lacked the executive presence she would need to move up within the organization. Because of her limited participation in meetings, many stakeholders didn't have a good "read" on her and her abilities. Although they heard about her great ideas and hard work, they never witnessed it in the meetings. Jane continued, "Natalie, you have a lot of potential and are doing a great job so far, but if you want to get to the next level in your career, you need to play a bigger role in meetings and showcase your talent."

Natalie had all the skills and experience to execute her new role. But she was not bringing these elements to bear in meetings, and that made her appear less able to do her job. Many leaders feel that if they put their heads down and do their job well, that's all that matters. Unfortunately, accomplishments in the role are not enough.

---

### YOUR MATRIX MOMENT: ELEVATING YOUR IMPACT IN MEETINGS

- Meetings, whether in person or virtual, are where most decisions in the matrix are made. This is the main stage!
- To ensure you maximize the important opportunities that meetings represent, spend time preparing for them. Reflect on the agenda and the participating stakeholders: What are their styles and priorities? Prepare your strategy and messaging in advance so that you are calm and poised in your delivery.
- Once you are in the meeting, make sure to select the right seat, participate appropriately, display confidence, use effective language, and demonstrate agility if things don't go as planned.
- After the meeting, complete the necessary next steps. Reflect on the discussions and the decisions, follow up on anything assigned to you, and circle back to your network to learn what they think about how it went. Address any issues that came up.
- Don't just show up! Your engagement in meetings is not only essential to your influencing efforts, it is also where you demonstrate your thought leadership and executive presence.

## MEETINGS AND EXECUTIVE
## PRESENCE ACTION PLAN

As you move into action planning, look at meetings not as roadblocks to your "real work" but as critical paths to innovation and collaboration in your organization. Remember, meetings have a greater impact in the matrix, and embracing that truth is a crucial element of matrix success.

We can't emphasize enough that the way you show up in meetings is of paramount importance to your success. Beware of the "Tyranny of the Urgent." Virtually every leader will agree to the principle that meeting preparation and executive presence are important, but then they get busy, do not take the time to prepare, and suffer the consequences. Scheduling the time is the best way to increase the odds that you do your preparation and are on top of your game for the meeting. Pencil in the block of time on your calendar and treat it as you would any other appointment. While we are not suggesting you do this for every meeting you attend, for the important ones we can guarantee it will be time well spent.

Think about an important meeting coming up, whether it is in person or virtual. With the skills and strategies provided earlier in this chapter in mind, answer the following questions:

1. **Before the meeting:** How will you prepare for the meeting? What do you know about the other participants? What is your objective in the meeting? What are the stakeholders' priorities?
2. **In the meeting:** Where are you going to sit? How and where do you plan to participate? What vocabulary do you plan to use to offer your opinions? What other strategies can help you participate appropriately and demonstrate your executive presence?
3. **After the meeting:** After the meeting is finished, what is your plan to complete the post-meeting checklist? Who will you contact from your network to debrief?

## A FINAL WORD ON MEETINGS

For many leaders, meetings feel like a necessary evil. You may take them for granted and simply wait for them to end. In reality, they are your greatest opportunity to drive your agenda and implement your ideas. In the matrix, meetings are where critical decisions are made. If you execute in each of the three key areas—preparation, performance in the meeting, and efficient follow-up—meetings will turn into an excellent platforms that you can use to optimize your impact and showcase your leadership.

# CHAPTER 8

❖

# Moving from Functional Expert to Strategic-Thought Partner

L ONG A PRIZED LEADERSHIP CAPACITY, strategic thinking is argu- ably one of the abilities that sets leaders on track for senior posi- tions. But, as is the case with many skills, the matrix raises the stakes. What's more, in the matrix, this kind of sophisticated thinking is called for much earlier in an executive's career. While in more hierar- chical organizations strategic thinking was the focus of senior leaders, in a highly integrated environment, leaders at the manager level are called upon to demonstrate this critical skill. In the matrix, accelerat- ing your learning curve is paramount when it comes to the art of stra- tegic thinking.

## THE IMPORTANCE OF STRATEGIC THINKING

One of the primary purposes of an integrated structure is to drive innovation through diversity of thought, and to leverage the benefits of creative thinking from a range of perspectives, on both the functional and the business side. This is what keeps the organization ahead of the competition and allows it to make decisions that anticipate consumer trends. This core purpose sparked leadership-competency models that emphasize mandates such as:

- cultivating an entrepreneurial mindset
- being a disruptive thinker
- being a thought leader
- demonstrating intellectual agility
- demonstrating outside-in thinking
- displaying transformational leadership
- becoming a strategic-thought partner

While many descriptors are used, all point to the same critical and yet elusive ability. We use the word *elusive* because, while strategic thinking is one of the most important differentiators for successful matrix leadership, it is also the one that creates the most confusion and, frankly, frustration.

Here's a conversation we have frequently as coaches in the matrix:

Client:   "We have a coaching need we would like to engage you on. Adrian has been an outstanding performer in our organization for the last twelve years, and we have recently promoted him to country manager. He has long excelled as an operator, and he also collaborates well with his peers. However, now that we are working in a more matrixed structure, we are asking all of our leaders to be more strategic in their approach, and this is not a strength Adrian has displayed. Can you work with him on strategic thinking?"

Us:   "Absolutely. We'd be happy to do that. Just to make sure we are aligned with your definition of *strategic thinking*, could you describe it? Can you give some examples of what, in Adrian's role, that type of thinking would look like?"

Client:   "Well . . . you know, just, he needs to take a step back. Look at things from ten thousand feet. Connect the dots."

Us:   "Yes, I get that from a conceptual standpoint. But can you tell me, for example, a specific project Adrian is working on now and how strategic thinking might have changed the way he's handled it? What would strategic thinking have looked like?"

Client:  "That's a good question. I can't give you an answer off-hand. It's just that he tends to see things purely from his business and the operational perspective, and we need him to have a broader lens."

Sound familiar? This common experience points to one of the inherent challenges in developing this next-level skill: *How to get really clear on what strategic thinking means from a behavioral standpoint.* Even very smart and sophisticated senior leaders who know all about the importance of being strategic struggle to define it in behavioral terms.

We have worked with hundreds of leaders for whom strategic thinking was the primary focus of their coaching and development plan. Frequently, when we asked them if they had been given the feedback they needed to expand their strategic thinking ability and whether they had been working to improve it, we heard some version of the following: "Sure, I have received feedback about becoming more strategic and, at a theoretical level, I think I understand what it's about. But I am not sure exactly what it means for real-time application. How do I do it in my day-to-day work?" How can you improve at something when you cannot clearly define it in terms of the behavior you need to demonstrate?

The second common challenge, arguably related to the first, is the notion that the capacity for strategic thinking is either innate or incredibly rare and difficult to develop. There's a widespread perception that a knack for strategic thinking is some kind of genetic gift you either have or you don't. Many people think that you need to have worked at a major consulting firm for years to develop this skill, and that if you spent most of your career excelling in your function or running a business, this kind of systems perspective is simply beyond your grasp. This line of thinking can be debilitating and demotivating, and it can prevent leaders from acquiring and strengthening this skill. In fact, strategic thinking is a capacity that can be developed, like any other. Which means that, with a real understanding of the muscles you need to strengthen, you can absolutely build this capacity if you commit the time and thus train wisely. As with any other area, some people are more naturally gifted than others, of course.

If you have had a role or a job that has given you exposure to and experience with strategic thinking, you have a head start. But, wherever you are in terms of your strategic abilities, you can get better. In this chapter, we dive into the how-to of developing and applying strategic thinking in real time.

One final dimension of strategic thinking, which is often underestimated, is perception. Many of the leaders we have coached shared a consistent frustration: "I understand that my leadership wants me to become a more strategic leader. What's frustrating is that I believe I *am* a strategic person, but they just don't see it." We are not suggesting it is fair; however, if you possess a brilliant strategic mind but you don't understand how to display it or you only share your strategic ideas with select audiences (rather than your most important stakeholders), you will *not* be perceived as a strategic person. As we will explore, with certain strategic thinking areas, 80 percent of the problem is that leaders do not know how to intelligently *demonstrate* the ability.

## SHOWCASING STRATEGIC THINKING

In this next section we will systematically break down the key components of strategic thinking. We have arrived at these five critical areas based largely on our own research and experience, having worked with hundreds of leaders for whom strategic thinking was the main development area. We uncovered many of these areas by having deep conversations with leaders and stakeholders, prompting them with specific questions until we arrived at the behavioral data that would position us and our coaching participants for success. These questions include:

- "If Joe's presentation had been more strategic in the way you had hoped, what would he have included that was missing? How could he have changed his focus?"

- "I understand that you felt Heather's perspective was too narrow. How would she have demonstrated to you that she had the broader lens you were hoping for?"
- "I hear you are asking Larissa to be more disruptive. Could you give me an example of what this kind of thinking would be in her business? What would it look like?"

Fortunately for us, the vast majority of senior leaders we interviewed patiently and intelligently delved in to give us a clearer picture of what strategic thinking looks like in their organizations. And, after having completed these coaching engagements successfully and witnessing what works and what doesn't, we have put together the behaviors senior leaders most consistently deemed as strategic and necessary for success.

In addition to describing each of the five skill areas, we provide an example of the skill's application from our coaching experience. Some are more robust case studies while others are general examples. Specific tips and techniques will help you strengthen these particular "muscles," while a range of tactics ensures you understand how to display the skill in such a way that your strategic contributions will be recognized and appreciated.

The five strategic thinking critical areas are:

1. Thinking with an enterprise-wide perspective
2. Showing macro and micro thinking
3. Developing a long-term focus
4. Fostering innovation
5. Looking around corners

## Demonstrate Enterprise-Wide Thinking

Arguably, the primary goal of a matrix leader is to be an enterprise-wide thinker, also known as a broad-based thinker or systems thinker. What this really means is that you've worked on your capacity to both understand and solve business challenges not only in your area of expertise and experience, but also from the perspectives of your stakeholders in different functions and parts of the business. You don't see the world exclusively through your function or business.

An enterprise-wide thinker has a grasp of how a particular proposal would influence different parts of the business, recognizing the impact and implications it may have on other functions. As such a thinker, your solutions are much more valuable because they address challenges in a complete and integrated way.

In addition to solving complex business problems, enterprise-wide thinking is an important way to build support, as it enhances your credibility with stakeholders. They realize that you understand all parts of the business and how they are connected. When you can communicate to stakeholders that you appreciate the needs of their function or business, you are better able to win their support.

We witnessed a success story in the arena of strategic thinking while working with the consumer insights team of a global consumer products company. As part of the matrix restructure, the global insights function was repositioned to operate as "internal strategic consultants" to influence the company's businesses around the globe regarding the regions, initiatives, and brands they should invest in.

The transition was a bumpy one. This was a role the company had previously paid a large consulting firm to handle. But now, in an effort to be more cost-efficient, the internal insights group picked up the responsibility. When the consulting firm handled this task, it had leverage and power because everyone knew the consultants cost a lot of money and that their report and findings would go directly to the CEO.

Our insights group, on the other hand, did not have that leverage. In fact, while they performed the same tasks the consultants had—gathering data, doing the analysis, and then offering their recommendations to business leaders around the world—the decision to implement the recommendations was ultimately left to the local business leaders. This meant that the success of the insights team was based on their ability to demonstrate their value and thought leadership to these local business leaders. They had to *sell* their insights to an internal audience.

This was a challenge that gave the insights group pause. In our first conversation, the team's leader told us, "My biggest concern is that we are going to look like classic technical experts. They are not going to take us seriously as strategic thought partners." The team's leader had observed that several of her team members, three of whom had PhDs in statistical analysis and had recently moved into their roles from academia, were communicating in ways that reinforced the technical-expert perception. They went deep into the numbers and data in their presentations, relied on highly technical consumer insights terminology, and failed to connect points back to the business and their local functional drivers.

This insights team faced the task of shifting the perception of the business leaders, who viewed the team's contributions as chiefly technical advice. Let's look at the process the insights team undertook to change the business leaders' opinion and assert themselves as strategic-thought partners.

Understanding the risk and the urgency, the insights team quickly realized that in order to influence their key stakeholders, they needed to deepen their understanding of the business context, the region, and the implications their recommendations would have. They needed to be more attuned to the experiences of the business leaders they hoped to influence.

Once the insights team had completed their thorough data analysis and arrived at their recommendations, they developed a plan to appeal to business leaders by undertaking the following:

1. **Make use of their networks.** The team created a map of all the key stakeholders within the businesses that they knew had influence and a deep knowledge base. Once the stakeholder map was finished, each insights team member shared his or her network, specifically the connections, with key stakeholders. Sometimes, these were existing direct relationships with the stakeholders while at other times the connection was a person in the team member's current network who could make an introduction to the stakeholder. Each insights team member committed to utilizing their network with the explicit purpose of increasing their understanding of the local business and the current challenges the stakeholders were facing.

2. **Identify the key influencers.** Because the team realized that leaders from the sales and marketing functions were particularly influential stakeholders, several members committed to tapping into their networks within sales and marketing to gain a deeper understanding of the function, the current focus areas, and the types of language these leaders used when discussing business issues.

3. **Learn about the influencers through meetings and research.** Insights team members requested that they be invited to a few sales and marketing meetings they wouldn't ordinarily have attended. This would provide them with valuable knowledge. They also researched and read popular sales and marketing articles and blogs to get a better feel for the way sales and marketing folks think. Certainly, their research did not make them full-blown subject-matter experts in marketing or sales, but this effort deepened their understanding considerably.

4. **Role-play and prepare.** After a couple of months attending sales and marketing meetings, researching, and gathering data, the consumer insights group reconvened and challenged themselves to think in a more enterprise-wide modality. They performed an exercise in which team members presented their recommendations to one another, and then to other members of the team who had developed in-depth knowledge of the stakeholders; these team members played devil's advocate, to help sharpen the presentation. They asked questions like, "How does the analysis line up with the current risks, challenges, and drivers of the local business?" "How would the sales and marketing leaders likely respond to those recommendations through their lenses and priorities?" and "Are we using the key language or vernacular that resonates with this group?" Based on these robust discussions, the team was able to develop presentations with recommendations and solutions that considered many of these elements.

The hard work of the insights team paid off. The response from the stakeholders after their presentation was positive. Feedback from business leaders to the SVP of consumer insights was highly encouraging, with comments including, "Your team surprised us in a positive way. We were expecting mostly their technical expertise but they clearly had been quite thoughtful about the broader context."

## How Do You Get Better at Enterprise-Wide Thinking?

As we can see from the consumer insights team, it is certainly possible to improve your enterprise-wide thinking, though it requires hard work, time, and patience. Here are some tips on how you can do it:

- Read the latest industry magazines and blogs related to the business/functional area you are targeting.
- Leverage network connections who are part of the relevant groups and teams to learn more about their fundamentals, priorities, and, vernacular.
- When appropriate, request to attend some of the functional or business internal meetings of the target group to learn more about the current priorities, hot buttons, and pain points, and to get a better sense of their vocabulary and communication style.

## How Do You Demonstrate Enterprise-Wide Thinking?

Finally, as we saw in our story, the consumer insights team not only did the requisite learning and data gathering to enhance their enterprise-wide thinking, they presented their information and asked the types of questions that exhibited this perspective. It's important to ask questions or make comments that demonstrate your understanding of the stakeholders' business and priorities. Questions the team asked stakeholders included:

- "Considering the current economic headwinds facing your country . . ."
- "Looking at the broader objectives you have of efficiencies and cost-cutting . . ."
- "Understanding the pressures you are facing from finance, our recommendation . . ."

## Show Your Understanding of the Micro and the Macro Picture

Developing the ability to see a situation from both a micro and a macro perspective will pay dividends on multiple levels. This is, in short, the capacity to demonstrate a deep understanding of the details of a particular business topic while simultaneously communicating how that depth and detail connect to the broad strategic perspective.

Here's an example: Cynthia was recently promoted to lead the sales organization of a financial services company. She was promoted largely because of her tremendous track record of success in sales, her positive energy, and the loyalty she inspired. She was also known for creativity and passion around continuous improvement, always challenging the team to generate more aggressive growth targets by trying new things. Cynthia's team members frequently said they would walk through fire for her. She was generally intuitive in her thinking, and company leadership was concerned about whether Cynthia could demonstrate the deep thinking and financial rigor required to develop an aggressive strategic plan that would increase sales by 15–20 percent. She needed to shift leadership's perception of her as merely a great salesperson and demonstrate her prowess as a true sales executive.

Cynthia diligently applied a micro and macro approach as she developed her strategic plan and always kept it top of mind when presenting to the senior leaders of the organization. She worked closely with the group CFO and other finance leaders, who challenged her to gain a deeper understanding of the numbers. "I need to distill all of the key facts in a succinct but detailed enough way that the SLT [senior leadership team] will be entirely confident with how I arrived at my strategic objectives. I want to demonstrate that my objectives are both innovative and disruptive while also realistic with measurable progress," she said.

Cynthia also developed a consistent presentation approach. She always led with her three major transformational strategic initiatives, showing aspirational goals and how these aligned with the company's three-year growth strategy. She would then pivot toward the detail that illuminated what these strategies and numbers were based on, providing a clear, metrics-driven explanation for how the company would achieve the goals and how progress would be measured. After several presentations and meetings over a few months, she became fluid and confident in her micro and macro approach and received excellent feedback.

Let's discuss the power of this ability to view goals from both macro and micro perspectives. First, it addresses the tension we commonly hear around the demand to think strategically and "elevate" rather than being tactical or "stuck in the weeds." However, we also hear consistently that senior leaders still want to know that you have a deep grasp of what is happening in your business or function, and that you have the data to support your position. While senior leaders vary in the granularity they are looking for, it is generally imperative that you are capable of backing up your assertions and plans with facts. We have certainly worked with leaders who are so focused on their high-level strategic thought that they were perceived as "up in the clouds" and "not grounded in reality," neither of which is a good thing.

By approaching your ideas in a micro and macro way, you can gain a high level of credibility with regard to your rigor and depth of knowledge *and* you can reinforce senior leaders' perception that you are a sophisticated strategic thinker. That is a truly powerful combination.

## How Do You Get Better at Micro and Macro Thinking?

The best way to strengthen your capacity to develop both micro and macro approaches depends on your natural inclinations. If you are more of a detail and numbers person, the stretch will be connecting that micro level to bigger-picture thinking. Paying close attention in internal meetings when the organization's global agenda and strategic priorities are being discussed can be particularly helpful.

If you are more of an ideas person, on the other hand, and tend to avoid taking the deeper dive, follow Cynthia's lead and immerse yourself in the specifics to make certain you connect to a way to make progress on the big goals. Who in the organization is naturally strong in the necessary functional areas and can help you develop a deeper understanding? Perhaps there is even someone you can delegate much of this task to. Whichever approach is your strength—micro or macro thinking— challenge yourself to present your strategic thinking in this holistic way.

*How Do You Demonstrate a Macro and Micro Approach?*

Cynthia's example beautifully captures how to display a micro and macro orientation. The key is to first capture the group's attention with the macro goal you are aiming to achieve; then share an overview of the strategy that will get you there and provide rigorous analysis and data that show why you are advocating for this strategy. Don't forget to include the data-driven processes you will have in place to measure success.

## Develop a Long-Term Focus

A close cousin to the micro and macro mindsets is the capacity to sustain a longer-term focus. Push yourself to plan for the long term—looking three to five years out—rather than adhering to the tactical, operational mindset concerned with this quarter or this fiscal year. This isn't always easy, because in most businesses there is tremendous pressure to deliver results right away. A lot of emphasis is put on the here and now.

But the ability to take the long view is a quality that senior leaders consistently point to as invaluable. Such strategic thinkers can demonstrate that they're not only looking at this year but have a long-range plan. What's more, they can articulate that longer-term plan in meetings. When long-term thinkers talk about current ideas they have, they present the short-term plan but also look ahead and view that initiative in the three- to five-year context. They're able to link current issues to those longer-term plans. The message to the audience is clear: this is somebody who thinks over the long term and not just in a tactical way geared for immediate results.

This kind of long-range thinking is commonly an "error of omission." When we coach individuals to develop this ability, we typically discover that they do have a long-term plan; they simply fail to share it consistently when in meetings with key stakeholder groups. Moreover, they often focus their presentations and discussions solely on the business in the near term.

*How Do You Get Better at Developing a Long-Term Focus?*

Reach out and gather all the information you can amass about your organization's long-term objectives. Also, employ the tools that make you so good at short-term focus for a long-term purpose. If you use calendars—real or virtual—to stay on task daily, look for ways to incorporate these into longer-term thinking. What is your one-year outlook? Three year? Five year? Get those concepts out of your head and into a format where you can consider them in a concrete and strategic way.

*How Do You Demonstrate a Long-Term Focus?*

To explain how you can demonstrate long-term thinking, we'll consider a real-life example. Emily, a senior director in finance, had received feedback about her lack of a long-term strategic vision. In our work with her, she acknowledged that her attention to detail and the pressure she was feeling to meet immediate business goals focused her exclusively on near-term execution. However, she accepted the feedback and committed to blocking off time to develop a longer-term plan. After investing several hours in planning over the course of a month, she felt good about the strategic vision she had developed. The next challenge was demonstrating her thinking. As Emily shared with us, "In meetings with my business and functional leaders, they do not usually specifically ask for my long-term vision or perspective. They just want me to report on what's happening now. How do I share this with them without it coming off as awkward or forced?" This is where a little creativity is warranted. We showed Emily that she could still report her numbers but then simply add a sentence or two related to the data that would demonstrate her long-term view. Examples included:

- "Based on the current numbers, this is going to position us for $X$ opportunity in twelve months . . ."
- "I wanted to highlight that if the trend of the current data continues, in eighteen months our margins will have increased to the point . . ."

- "Based on my analysis, the current numbers indicate that if we stay consistent, within two years we will erase the competitive advantage $X$ competitor has had on us recently . . ."
- "Our current numbers being where they are, as we look toward the future, this is going to give us a platform to establish $X$ in the next three years . . ."

She was still providing the data requested but found creative ways to incorporate the long-term vision she had manifested. Within just a few months of consistently sharing her ideas this way in key meetings, senior leaders' perception of her abilities began to shift in a positive direction.

## Foster Innovation

Innovation is another common theme in the area of strategic thinking. It can be a loaded subject because when people hear the word *innovator*, they immediately think of Steve Jobs, Bill Gates, or Henry Ford. You might be saying to yourself, "I'm not an inventive genius like these people. I doubt that I will have an Einstein moment where I will suddenly reinvent or entirely disrupt our industry."

A small percentage of individuals has been blessed with an exceptional ability to innovate. If you are one of these, congratulations. However, even if you do not put yourself in that category, you can still become meaningfully innovative in your own right. While this skill, at its core, is about creativity, it is also about curiosity, open-mindedness, risk-taking, and a drive for continuous improvement.

Here is a perfect example: We coached an IT leader in a large telecommunications company. The company was having issues with a service function that wasn't performing properly. Customers complained that the problem was impacting their service and it needed to be fixed ASAP. This IT leader approached the problem very methodically. Keeping an open mind about the possible root causes, he interviewed multiple team members, from product managers to senior engineers to quality-assurance folks to those in customer implementation. He gathered all the data and began testing different scenarios. At last, he found the cause of the problem and was able to develop a solution. Not only was he able to solve the initial problem, the new application he designed actually enhanced the function, improving the overall quality of the service. The company's senior leaders and his team members were impressed. They called him an innovator and lauded his great ideas and creativity. While he enjoyed the kind words, he knew that he only achieved this success by keeping an open mind about the potential problem, showing curiosity, asking questions, testing multiple theories, and driving for improvement. His innovation did not come via a genius Einstein-type moment but through a carefully crafted inquiry.

### How Can You Get Better at Innovating?

Innovation begins with a mindset and an orientation. The mindset is one of perpetual curiosity, of not settling for the status quo; the orientation is one of continuous exploration, of inviting new and different ways of doing things. Do you consistently ask yourself, "How can we do things differently? What industry best practices can we apply?" One key way to foster innovation is to get out of your own bubble and connect with the world around you. You may see an idea you can adapt, or the experience of connection may spark an entirely new idea to try. Both these approaches are engines of innovation. True innovators are interacting with other thinkers all the time. Go to trade shows and industry conferences to see what other companies are trying and what current thought leaders are speaking about. Study the competition: What is working for them and where are they spinning their wheels? Read industry trade publications and blogs. Innovation is a conversation taking place in all these spaces, and you can harness that energy by getting into the mix yourself.

Finally, don't forget to leverage the innovative ideas of your team and peers. Simply by posing the aforementioned questions, you may discover that colleagues around you have brilliant ideas that haven't been heard. A leader who *fosters* and encourages an open space for innovation is often just as valuable as one who dreams up brilliant plans on her own.

*How Can You Demonstrate Your Ability to Innovate?*

First, simply by challenging the team to think about ways to improve, you show that you are not someone who wants to stay in a comfort zone. You are curious. You are a person who is always looking for ways your business can evolve.

However, if you're the leader who often says, "We've tried that," "That'll never work," or "Here is the problem with that," you may be reinforcing a perception that you shut things down and block innovative thinking. That impression can certainly hurt you. Find opportunities in meetings to share insights you have learned from your reading or advances you gleaned from an industry conference of the latest best-in-class processes the organization may be able to apply.

Do not feel like the only innovation worth sharing must be earth-shattering. If you designed a more efficient way to prorate workflows or came up with a new system to organize data, share it! Remember, the matrix process of leveraging best practices may transform what you consider a small innovation into a really valuable idea that can be applied in other parts of the organization.

## Get Good at Looking Around Corners

Another powerful strategic thinking concept is what is known as *looking around corners*. It's not unique to the matrix environment. Arguably, this is what the top leaders of any organization are paid to do. That said, this brand of insight has particular power in the matrix, where high-level strategic thinking is at a premium throughout the organization, not just in the most senior ranks. Looking around corners means anticipating consumer trends in a way that takes into account turns in the path and doesn't assume the future will unfold in a series of straight-line innovations. It speaks to the capacity to think ahead and predict changes in popular tastes and preferences. To quote a business truth, "Change is the only constant." The goal of this kind of thinking is to anticipate shifts and make strategic decisions now to position the business to seize that change successfully.

One of our coaching clients who excels at looking around corners described her process in the following way: "I am always studying the marketplace for consumer trends, both inside and outside our industry. The goal is to try to understand what is going to motivate our consumer to make decisions in the future, in a way that is different from today. Where decisions may have been driven purely by efficiency, cost, health, or taste in the past, in the future it may be more about the experiences the products create. Does it create joy? Is it connected to a core value they believe in? Then, of course, convenience, speed, and ease of use also matter, which is often where technology plays a role."

When you can identify and predict marketplace changes, you are looking around corners. A strategic thinker in the matrix organization encourages and models this practice. This leader says, "Here are the things we need to do today in order to position ourselves for the new trends that will take hold tomorrow."

Jeff Bezos's creation of Amazon is arguably the most successful example of looking around corners, as he anticipated the convergence of technology and consumers' desire for convenient shopping. Many grocery stores and restaurants have seen similar trends related to delivery, with customers choosing digital kiosks for speed and efficiency.

Marketing is another area that has seen a significant shift, this time away from the traditional model that emphasized TV commercials to a more modern approach focused on social media, internet ads, and mobile advertising. Those leaders who are intentionally looking toward the future and disrupting the way business is done position their organizations to capitalize on change.

### How Do You Get Better at Looking Around Corners?

Many of the skills we talked about in the innovation section apply to looking around corners as well. However, if innovation is a skill that chiefly solves a near-term problem, looking around corners contemplates the longer-range view. Innovation is the spark that fuels the next quarter; looking around corners engages in work that will come five to ten years down the road and beyond.

*How Do You Demonstrate Looking Around Corners?*

As with innovation, the key to showing that you have an eye to the distant future is to have the *decent boldness* to share your thinking. If you look around the corner and think of an idea that merits discussion, take the time to build a presentation around it. Not only will this force you to ensure you have been truly thoughtful about your strategy, it will also challenge you to show in more concrete ways the upside and the impact it can have on the business. Then, have the decent boldness to share your presentation. Perhaps start one-on-one with peers you trust from your network, and if you get positive feedback and encouragement, ask for some time on the meeting agenda.

Lean in and take a risk. In our experience—assuming there is no major political fallout to what you are suggesting—these efforts are appreciated, as organizations are looking for their people to step up and guide the company's future. If your idea gets traction, you may have a considerable impact on the organization; if it is appreciated but not acted upon at this time, you have still demonstrated that you're a strategic thinker who has this capacity.

## CARVE OUT TIME FOR STRATEGIC THINKING

In addition to coaching individuals, we also frequently work with leadership teams to support their optimal performance. We generally begin these engagements with interviews that help us learn, among other things, what the team is doing well and what they could do better. In most cases, strategic thinking is one of the major themes in the improvement bucket. One comment we hear often from these leaders is, "We all know we should be doing more strategic thinking—in fact, we are the ones telling our teams that they should be doing more of it as well. But it seems like we are going from one fire drill to the next without ever having time to do the strategic thinking!" Sound familiar?

Yet, the reality is that some leaders are demonstrating strategic thinking fairly regularly, and they work in the same crazy busy world you do. This means they have made a conscious decision to carve out time for strategic reflection. They understand that quality strategic thought rarely happens when we are harried, scattered, and multitasking. It requires a span of calm (ideally uninterrupted), during which you can think and reflect.

We encourage you to be proactive and block time on your calendar every month for strategic thinking. Remember this wise expression when it comes to prioritizing your time: "If you don't have a plan for your time, somebody else will." In other words, if you do not protect the time you need to strengthen your ability to think strategically, someone is certain to schedule a meeting or take up your time in some other way.

Another useful phrase to remember is, "Every time I say yes to something, I am saying no to something else." When you are busy, every decision about how you use your time—whether it is an intentional choice or not—is a trade-off. Be careful you are not saying no to strategic thinking time because you say yes to everything else.

---

### YOUR MATRIX MOMENT: MOVING FROM FUNCTIONAL EXPERT TO STRATEGIC-THOUGHT PARTNER

- Strategic thinking is not an ability you either have or you don't. It is a skill like any other, and you can improve it.
- Focus on the five critical strategic thinking areas: enterprise-wide perspective, macro vs. micro thinking, long-term focus, innovation, and looking around corners.
- Recognize the importance of demonstrating your ability to think strategically to others within your organization. Unless you purposefully show your strategic thinking, key stakeholders may not be aware that you possess this invaluable skill.
- In a busy environment, it is easy for strategic thinking time to get squeezed. Make sure you schedule time to work on this area.

## CREATING YOUR STRATEGIC-THINKING ACTION PLAN

An essential part of getting better as a strategic thinker is reflecting on your current ability, considering how you are perceived, and then deciding what actions you will employ to improve. Reflect on your current abilities for each of the strategic-thinking skills: enterprise-wide thinking, micro and macro approach, long-term thinking, innovation, and looking around corners. Ask yourself:

- What score would you give yourself on the skill, on a scale from 1–10?
- How do you think you are perceived, on a scale of 1–10?
- What strategies can you employ to improve this skill?

Look at the reflections you have worked through and at the activities you identified that will strengthen your strategic thinking.

- Which two activities do you see as most important?
- What actions will you commit to (and protect) on your calendar to ensure they will happen?

## A FINAL WORD ON STRATEGIC THINKING

Strategic thinking is something all organizations look for in their leaders, yet most organizations are unable to clearly define what it means. As a result, few leaders receive the specific and actionable feedback that helps them develop this critical capacity. But the ability to think strategically and demonstrate your thinking within your organization is something you can learn and practice. Use the five key areas—enterprise-wide perspective, macro vs. micro thinking, long-term focus, innovation, and looking around corners—as your compass in this area. Finally, don't underestimate the importance of perception. It's not enough to simply be a strategic thinker; you need to show it. Make sure you demonstrate your skills in a clear and visible way.

# CHAPTER 9

❖

# Demonstrating Cultural Savvy

I N A MARKETPLACE that prizes global reach, you'd be hard-pressed to find a leader in any industry who will acknowledge a lack of cultural savvy. Indeed, this is considered a baseline skill that everyone in a leadership role must have, and the absence of cultural dexterity would be considered a grave deficit by any thinking leader.

Yet, even as a deep understanding of various cultures—whether these are national, regional, or organization-based—is prized, many leaders are surprisingly poor at demonstrating their cultural awareness in a matrix context. In today's extraordinarily global experience, well-intentioned leaders frequently make consequential missteps such as communicating in ways that create misunderstandings or behaving in a manner that disrespects cultural norms. Although our consulting practice is based in the US, we have worked almost as much outside North America as we have inside it, completing hundreds of coaching assignments and several hundred leadership programs in more than twenty countries across all continents. As a result, this topic is one with which we have decades of firsthand knowledge.

Cultural savvy is not a once-in-a-while practice—quite the opposite. The impact of cultural issues is vast and often plays a role in every interaction within the organization, as well as with vendors and customers. That's because culture is more than race or ethnicity. Culture is the word we use to describe the norms and behaviors of any given group. And those norms may vary by country or continent, as we've all been schooled to expect, but they can also vary greatly from one division to another, or one function to the next. Add to these variables, which already create a rich mix of cultural differences, the dynamics created by mergers and acquisitions, which frequently bring disparate cultures together. Because of the highly integrated nature of the matrix, there may be considerable cultural differences not only within the same geography but even within the same building. We've seen cultures vary from floor to floor. Cultural difference is not a factor to be underestimated.

Most large companies today are facing that reality. In global matrix organizations, anyone with a global role (a large percentage of the organization) must consistently engage and collaborate with stakeholders from other regions, countries, and parts of the world. And, while every organization certainly has programs related to the importance of being inclusive and respectful of cultural diversity, that messaging has not solved the problem of culture clashes for many matrix leaders. There are certain dimensions of cultural savvy that global matrix leaders can very easily miss, and this is more than a small problem.

As we have conveyed throughout this book, maintaining trust, credibility, and positive, respectful relationships is critical to any successful matrix collaboration, and all of these requirements are impacted greatly by the give and take of culture-infused interactions. The level of sensitivity with regard to culture can be either a powerful enabler of these global relationships or a major derailer, depending upon how well that sensitivity is exercised. Cultural savvy, in other words, can tip a project toward success or failure.

One piece of good news is that technology is stepping into the arena of cultural awareness in a robust way. The internet, as well as many useful apps and other tech tools, allows you to quickly find valuable information about holiday schedules, customs, cultural history, and general behavioral norms, and we certainly advocate leveraging these useful resources. However, even with these resources available, we often hear in our individual coaching and leadership development work about US-centric leaders who create frustration and suffer a loss of credibility when engaging with their global counterparts because they lack basic awareness. We have witnessed many scenarios in which leaders from different regions and countries created conflict, broke trust, and undermined their own credibility as they engaged with their counterparts across continents, within continents, and even within countries. The cultural savvy issue is real, and while technology solutions help, they have not erased the problem.

Clearly, culture is a rich and complex topic that could fill volumes. As with all the topics in this book, however, we've boiled the how-to component of each skill down to its essence. With that goal, we identified four core areas where a lack of understanding can most easily lead to interactions that damage positive relationships:

1. Communication norms
2. The way decisions get made
3. Common values and taboos
4. The global mindset

If you can address these four topics in the context of cultural differences and apply what you've learned, you will be primed to navigate the complexity of the matrix. If you leave one of these out of your skill set, you are more than likely headed for a challenge—and the challenge can arise more quickly than you might imagine. Before we dive into the specifics of acquiring cultural savvy, we'll review the potential consequences that failing to adapt to cultural contexts can yield.

## CASE STUDY: A LACK OF CULTURAL SAVVY CAN SINK YOU

Jenny Chow had recently been promoted to director of global consumer insights for a pharmaceutical company based in the Netherlands. Jenny started her career in management consulting in Asia, working mainly in Tokyo, Hong Kong, and Shanghai for six years before developing a passion for consumer insights. After going to grad school and completing her MBA, she was hired by the pharmaceutical company's Hong Kong office, which was also their regional HQ. Jenny progressed quickly up the ranks and was promoted to director within six years, assessed by the organization as having the potential to rise several more levels in seniority.

The pharmaceutical company had recently reorganized to a highly integrated matrix structure. As part of their reorganization, they created a new department called Global Insights for the Future, which would be based at the HQ in Amsterdam and have as its exclusive focus anticipating future consumer trends and helping to shape the organization's vision for the future. The talent team identified Jenny as an ideal candidate to join the group. Not only would she bring her strong track record and talent, she would also be exposed to HQ and work more closely with leaders there.

Excited about the opportunity, Jenny moved her family and was ready for her new adventure. Naturally, she was aware that the Dutch culture was different from her native culture in many ways. She had visited HQ at least twice a year for the previous four years for global meetings, and she felt she was prepared to make the adjustments.

By nature a highly analytical person, Jenny liked to take time to formulate her thoughts. In addition, as a result of her cultural background, she was fairly modest and low on her need for attention as well as more deferential to senior leaders. Furthermore, Jenny had been taught to communicate in a polite and indirect way when giving her opinion. As a result of her cultural disposition, when Jenny attended meetings with senior leaders at HQ, she would underparticipate relative to her peers; when she did feel comfortable enough to give her input, she did that much later in the meeting. As a result of her style, she appeared tentative and used qualifying language when giving her opinion, even though in her mind she was communicating her ideas very clearly.

Jenny was particularly reluctant to challenge or push back on ideas being discussed in meetings out of fear of creating conflict, a state vastly out of her comfort zone. When she did look to drive her ideas forward, she spent most of her time in individual meetings influencing her own boss rather than gaining input from and alignment with her peers on the team. This would have been an appropriate strategy in Jenny's former roles in Asia, where decisions were made in a more top-down, hierarchical fashion.

The challenge for Jenny was that Dutch culture was very different from her native culture in virtually every way, and her attempt to adapt did not go nearly far enough. The Dutch communication style is famously direct, to the point that people are sometimes described as communicating in a very "Dutch" way. In addition, the Dutch in general—and this organization in particular—pride themselves on healthy debate. At HQ, leaders at all levels were expected to be comfortable challenging one another—and this included challenging "up" and disagreeing with senior leaders. Finally, the decision-making approach in the Netherlands was highly inclusive, with everyone on the team expected to give input and be part of the decision-making process, not just the senior leader.

Six months into her new role, Jenny was in trouble. Her boss scheduled time with her for a feedback discussion. The conversation was tough love, to say the least, with Jenny getting the following feedback: "We all understand you are not only new to the role, but also very new to the culture so we wanted to give you some time to get comfortable and settled in over the last few months. However, we are observing certain behaviors that are concerning to us. First, we were so excited to have you on this team because we have heard about and seen your track record of innovation and excellent insights and analysis, which really impacted the business in our Asia market. However, since you have been here, we feel there has been a real absence of your thought leadership and impact. In addition, we are concerned that you may not be comfortable challenging others' ideas and the status quo, which has us wondering if you are always fully sharing what's on your mind. Finally, your approach to influencing has left many of us wondering whether you are a true team player."

We have highlighted this case study because, in this example, the cultural differences were so significant that they touched on three of the four key areas we have set out as critical (all but global mindset). We could have chosen dozens of similar case studies and named dozens, if not hundreds, of examples that include just one of these core areas, and which had a negative impact on relationships, collaboration, and organizational effectiveness. In many instances, they also had a detrimental effect on the individual's career progression. The stories are almost end-less, but the connecting factor is the same: The consequences of flawed cultural understanding are significant and often swift.

## HOW TO ACQUIRE CULTURAL SAVVY: COVER THE FOUR KEY BASES

Cultural savvy is a vast skill, and one that any individual could spend a lifetime perfecting. To avoid becoming overwhelmed, start with the four basic concepts—communication norms, decision-making norms, common values and taboos, and the global mindset—and then build from that base. If you're working in a situation that involves multiple cultures (and, as we've pointed out, that can involve anything from multiple countries to several floors of one office building), begin with these "minimums" and then keep your eyes and ears open to learn more nuance as your stakeholder relationships grow.

A recurring theme of this book is that successful matrix leadership begins with the right attitude and orientation: cultural savvy is no dif-ferent. The following mantra captures the spirit we encourage leaders to embrace: "I have chosen to work for an organization that is great in large part because of the cultural diversity and global reach we have. No culture is better or worse or right or wrong; they are simply differ-ent. Because I value this diversity, I make it a priority to educate myself about these cultures, learn about their norms and values, and ensure that I engage with my colleagues in a respectful way." Reminding yourself of these realities regularly inculcates a sense of acceptance, encouraging you to see the value cultural diversity brings and motivating you to pri-oritize this capacity.

Another delicate but important topic in enabling cultural dexter-ity concerns stereotypes and stereotyping. When you begin generalizing about any global or company culture, you naturally run the risk of portray-ing it inaccurately. Not only do exceptions to every stereotype exist, but each individual in each country is entirely unique in his or her own right.

There is such a thing, however, as *useful* generalization. A broad view does, at a minimum, provide a helpful starting place or frame when engaging with stakeholders who are not part of your native culture, division, or business area. The norms and impressions that have fed stereotypes are typically rooted in mass experience. When you hear guidance such as, "Germans are usually very direct in their communication" or "That part of the organization dresses informally" or "Brazilians are highly relationship driven," that information has, generally, been established based on accumulated data and observation. Therefore, we do encourage you to learn about these important norms—they can give you an informed starting place for the way you engage, rather than just showing up in your natural comfort zone and hoping for the best. If, over time, you discover that the individuals you are collaborating with do not fit the cultural frame you'd expected, adjust your behavior accordingly.

Commit to doing your homework: it is through active research that you will discover valuable cultural knowledge about four critical areas. In the following sections, we explore each of these topic areas, how you can discover this information, and how to adapt your behavior accordingly.

Remember, too, the invaluable source of information that resides in your network. Gaining insights directly from those who are part of the cultures/teams/functions you are working with is always your best option.

## Understanding Communication Norms

When it comes to differences in communication style, there is plenty of common sense but not much in the way of common practice. Most leaders working for global companies would be able to articulate the importance of adapting to different communication norms, yet mistakes happen constantly.

As an example, let's look at two norms we call *direct* and *indirect communication*, sometimes expressed as *aggressive* and *polite*. These are two very different styles of expression, and various cultures may lean toward one end of the extreme or the other, or may fall somewhere along the continuum. Our reaction to a communication norm that differs from our own can be visceral and emotional, and may result in a response that impacts trust and credibility. An individual with a direct communication style can be perceived as disrespectful, pushy, and abrasive. On the flip side, indirect communicators may be tagged as lacking confidence, wishy-washy, or conflict averse. This is a pervasive challenge in a global matrix because countries' position along the spectrum from direct to indirect communication can be dramatically different. For example, leaders from the Netherlands, Germany, Russia, Turkey, Australia, France, and the US Northeast tend to have a direct communication style. Meanwhile, leaders from Thailand, Japan, Vietnam, the UK, Ireland, and New Zealand lean toward a more polite or indirect orientation. Leaders and teams on each end of the spectrum might very well come away from an interaction with the emotional response that the other side is "doing it wrong."

How do you approach this issue? Investigate the traditional communication norms of societies around the world, and consider communication norms in other contexts, such as in different departments or divisions of the same company. The norm is really whatever the tradition has become in that stakeholder community. When you understand how people in a particular group are used to communicating, you can adapt your style accordingly to build connection and support. It's not that your original communication style is bad or wrong—it may simply be different from that of the stakeholders you seek to engage. By adapting, you not only show cultural savvy, you demonstrate a willingness to work across boundaries and create a positive relationship. Just as locals appreciate tourists learning a few key phrases of their language, stakeholders recognize and appreciate your efforts.

Keep in mind that communication norms do not apply only to in-person speech. Today, we communicate in a variety of ways and with the assistance of more than one technology platform. As you research your stakeholder audience, ask questions that pertain to technological communication. What kind of information is shared via email? Via text? In which cases is a phone call preferred? When must something be committed to old-fashioned paper? And when will only a face-to-face conversation do? These are all elements of communication that are heavily influenced by cultural norms. When dealing with the hot, new startup in Silicon Valley, leaders might be annoyed to find you called a full in-person meeting to discuss a new product idea. That stakeholder group might be perfectly comfortable brainstorming virtually via group chat. On the other hand, an effort to use email to schedule an important meeting with senior stakeholders in an old-line industrial firm might fall apart, since that culture relies on human senior assistants to act as calendar keepers. Knowing how your stakeholders view each communication form is part of understanding their norms.

No matter what format you're using—technology, paper, or face-to-face, remember to use the vocabulary and phrasing of executive communication we discussed in chapter 6, "Honing Advanced Communication Skills." As you will recall, we provided a range of vocabulary designed to help you calibrate the directness of your communication for optimal impact. These battle-tested words and phrases will keep you in good standing with your stakeholders and save you a lot of frustration.

When you take the time to learn and adapt to stakeholders' communication norms, you telegraph a position of respect and interest. This is a smart way to put colleagues in their comfort zone and avoid misunderstandings.

## Recognizing Decision-Making Norms

Who makes the decisions in the stakeholder group, and how are they made? Decision-making is another dimension that can trip up leaders in a matrix. We discussed the importance of understanding power dynamics and decision-making in chapter 5; now we want to highlight how important culture issues can be in the decision-making process.

Perhaps the most common cultural split with regard to decision-making revolves around whether decisions are: a) collaborative in nature, in which a broad group of the team influences the decision, or b) top-down, in which power resides at the top of the hierarchy. This is a particularly important topic across regions because people in diverse parts of a country or the world are used to different approaches and have varied expectations. For instance, in the US and many western European countries, the expectation is that decisions are made quite collaboratively—everybody weighs in and has the potential to influence the decision. Clearly, there is a leader with seniority who may make a final call, but the fundamental expectation is that the process of getting to the final decision is collaborative and consensus oriented.

Contrast that style with the more hierarchical approach common in countries such as India, China, and Russia. Those countries are far more likely to have a top-down decision-making norm as part of the culture.

When leaders and stakeholders accustomed to one decision-making norm are confronted with a contrasting style, things can go sideways quickly. The situation may play out something like this: Our matrix leader from the Netherlands reaches out to stakeholders in India. He has long been successful in consensus-built decision-making, the norm in his local workplace. Now our matrix leader is prepared to use his tried-and-true strategies with this new group in India. He consults the organization chart of the India-based stakeholder group and uses it to guide his path. "These are all the people I need to speak with," he surmises. "So I'll set up meetings and try to influence them and get their buy-in."

Our matrix leader devotes a good deal of time to this process, working his way through the org chart, setting up meetings, conducting influencing sessions, seeking buy-in from these stakeholders. Three months in, he recognizes that, despite his best efforts, he doesn't appear to be getting any traction. Checking his notes, he can see he's often getting one response on the conference call or in a meeting—lots of head nodding—but that agreement doesn't lead to a decision.

After a lot of work and frustration, our US-based matrix leader finally figured out he was making a cultural mistake. To gain traction with his India-based stakeholder group, he could not rely on the consensus tactics that had served him well in Amsterdam. Instead, he had to consider the top-down norm of decision-making in this new context. He needed to seek out the senior leader of that stakeholder group and learn what that individual cared about—and how to get his own project onto that leader's agenda. That was the individual who could make the decision that would ultimately drive the work of the full stakeholder team. The India-based team would rely on that norm and wait for that individual to make a decision. Without that person's buy-in, our Netherlands-based leader was spinning his wheels.

This is a case in which the failure to appreciate a top-down culture held up the project. The flip side is also quite common. When a leader with a norm for top-down behavior brings that tactic to a culture that is more consensus-based, hackles are sure to rise. Let's say a Russia-based leader, who is accustomed to a norm of top-down decision-making, comes to a UK stakeholder group and seeks out the team leader, not bothering to engage the full team. That is how things are done, in our Russia-based leader's experience. But in the UK, the response may be negative. By spending time influencing the senior leader and not involving the other stakeholders, our Russia-based leader could be seen as political and lacking in collaborative spirit.

Knowing the decision-making norms of the stakeholders you're approaching is a critical culture check. Not all companies in a country or region are the same, but knowing the prevalent expectations and norms will help you navigate the new territory without making unnecessary culture mistakes.

## Know the Values and Taboos

Values present an even trickier landscape to navigate than decision-making or communication norms. This is the case because differences in values are more likely to create experiences that feel personal. Whether the difference is between self-promotion and humility or task orientation versus relationship orientation in the workplace, a failure to appreciate differences in values can not only lead to a basic disconnect, it touches emotional hot buttons and can feel like a personal affront. Further, many of the values and taboos fall into the category of unwritten rules, which increases the likelihood that we will miss them if we are not intentional about discovering them. Considering the importance of this dimension, we encourage you to reach out to your network early on to gain as much insight as possible. Some of the questions you may use to respectfully ask questions about cultural norms and taboos include:

- "I'm really excited to be partnering with your global team on this project, in part because it will be my first opportunity to work with your country and culture. With that in mind, it is a priority for me to ensure I always communicate and behave in a way that will be deemed courteous and respectful. I would really appreciate any advice you have about important 'do's and don'ts' so that I can achieve that goal."

- "I would really appreciate your guidance on some of the most common cultural mistakes you have seen other leaders from my part of the world (or organization) make when engaging with your team from the standpoint of your core norms and values—I want to do my best to avoid them if possible!"

It's critical to understand the unwritten rules of any stakeholder group. Without this knowledge, a well-intentioned matrix leader might inadvertently offend, disrespect, or simply behave in a way that negatively impacts how she is perceived. Many different types of values and taboos exist in any given group; we'll address some of the most common trip wires here.

*Relationship Orientation*

People living in different countries or regions can perceive and value relationships in diverse ways. For example, people in Latin American countries are famous for their high-touch relationship values, and they place tremendous importance on the process of connecting in person and developing strong connections. By contrast, those in countries such as Germany, Russia, and other northern European nationalities tend to be far more task-oriented in the work environment, placing less emphasis on the need to connect and bond interpersonally. This can be tricky to navigate, particularly for matrix leaders, who may toggle between countries that have leaders and teams with differing relationship-orientation views.

We once worked with a leader who was born in Brazil, studied at Harvard, and then went on to work in the US. He was often schooled to shift his relationship orientation, and told, "Remember, this is not the same as Latin America, where work relationships are fostered on person-to-person friendships and time investment." Then, after a decade in the

US, this leader went back to Brazil, where he was now perceived as aloof and impersonal. The moral is that neither relationship style is wrong; it is incumbent upon the leader to remember where he is, learn the local relationship orientation values and taboos, and adjust accordingly.

*Self-Promotion vs. Humility*

If you are based in the US, the following is of particular importance to you because the values and taboos around self-promotion and humility often rise up as hurdles when a US-based leader tries to connect with an Asia-based stakeholder. Why are we singling out the US? In our experience, if you ask a global audience to name a country that is comfortable with its own greatness (and shares that with others), the quickest answer is: the United States. It's not good or bad, it's simply what it is. In light of this reality, US leaders need to understand their own values and taboos and recognize the contrasting style they may encounter.

Many cultures in the world—classically, Japan, Thailand, and other Asian countries—pride themselves on humility. Being humble is viewed as positive and the opposite—trying to stand out—is considered taboo. A popular expression in many of these countries is, "The nail that sticks out gets hammered."

This value system has significant impact on the best approach. For example, if a New Yorker went to a meeting in Japan but presented his traditional "New York" stance to strongly advocate for his position and self-promote to establish his credibility, his behavior could easily alienate stakeholders.

The opposite negative impact also holds true. As we saw in the case study, when a leader schooled in the self-effacing values of Asia is immersed in a different cultural context, the negative impact of his behavior can be significant.

*Positivity*

A positive outlook is another value that can be a stumbling block for global matrix leaders, and it's one that often pits the US against the world. The US is famous for its optimistic orientation. We can do it!

Everything is going great! This will be a big hit! Leaders in the UK, Germany, and the Netherlands tell stories of eye-rolling and frustration when they interact with their US counterparts, who always tell them that everything is terrific, everything's fantastic, everything's wonderful. This is not the way the European leaders were trained to think. And US leaders who insist on relentless positivity may lose credibility with their international colleagues.

When positivity meets a differing cultural value, the results can be dismaying. Let's consider our US leader making a connection with stakeholders in Germany. The US leader is optimistic about the project thus far, and is even more confident about its outlook for the future. This positivity radiates from every interaction, be it in person, on a conference call, or via a virtual platform.

Meanwhile, the German-trained leader comes to the project with a different set of values. In this leader's experience, the best way forward is to meet an idea, tear the idea to pieces, and then see if there's anything left to work with it. It is a brutal trial by inquiry that will seem smart and prepared to the German-based stakeholders but unnecessarily grim to US leaders. This clash of values can create great frustration on both sides. Both may telegraph a lack of credibility. But the truth remains that if you don't understand the cultural context you're working within and you interact based entirely on your own norms, you could be perceived as either a naïve optimist or a negative small thinker. Recognizing the values around positivity in advance allows you to calibrate your presentation to suit the listening stakeholders and build buy-in.

### Relationship with Authority

Varying attitudes with respect to authority is a difference that has been touched on in other cultural discussions, but it bears repeating here. When you are working in a culture different from your own, you need to know how that culture feels about authority. In some cases, deference to a senior leader is expected, whether it's in the context of major decision-making or who speaks at the meeting. The flip side is a culture that encourages debate and inquiry, with senior leadership that expects other leaders to speak up, challenge ideas, and engage in healthy public debate. Between these two extremes you may find combinations of these cultural preferences. The key is to understand how leadership is viewed in particular stakeholder groups, so take the time to learn how deference to authority is handled, and you will avoid hitting this cultural roadblock.

### Demonstrate a Global Mindset

A global mindset is critical only if you are working in a global organization. When you are part of a global matrix partnership, remember to present your ideas and recommendations in a way that demonstrates your global mindset or lens. Refrain from:

- Creating presentation decks that use mostly data, examples, and application from within your local business, country, or region. This can quickly turn off your global partners and hurt your credibility with them, even if your overall concept would be helpful.
- Using language and phrasing that is colloquial or idiomatic, and thus unfamiliar to nonnative speakers.
- Offering examples or anecdotes related to the value of your ideas based on your region alone. Local anecdotes are useful, as long as they are accompanied by global examples. You may think your cache of stories builds your case, but if the examples all represent the same region or culture, they may do exactly the opposite of what you intend.

## CREATING YOUR CULTURAL SAVVY ACTION PLAN

Before we discuss the action plan, we would like to revisit the case study from earlier in the chapter regarding Jenny, the struggling transplant to the Dutch office. Hopefully, her approach to remedying her behavior will offer a helpful template for change.

---

### YOUR MATRIX MOMENT:
### DEMONSTRATING CULTURAL SAVVY

- Understanding cultural differences is a critical component of leading in a matrix, whether these differences are arising across departments, regions, or countries. Factor in culture when collaborating with others.
- Make sure to cover the four key bases of demonstrating cultural savvy:

  1. Understand communication norms
  2. Recognize decision-making norms
  3. Know the values and taboos
  4. Demonstrate a global mindset

- Do your homework and be ready to adapt your approach to ensure positive relationships with stakeholders working within differing cultural contexts.

---

After providing Jenny with feedback that she was underparticipating in meetings, failing to challenge others enough, and not influencing as they had hoped, the company engaged a coach to support Jenny as she integrated into her new role. Fortunately, she was open to the feedback and to incorporating the learning we have shared throughout this chapter. She changed her approach to the way she showed up in meetings, increasing her participation earlier in meetings, using more assertive language, and developing the mindset and skill set to respectfully challenge others' thinking (including senior leaders). She also adapted her influencing approach to be more inclusive and consensus driven.

Ultimately, cultural issues are a critical element to matrix leadership. So much of what we do involves reaching across boundaries—be they national, ethnic, or departmental—so bridging culture gaps is likely a constant part of our leadership efforts. The key to success is to remember that culture will not be ignored. Navigating cultural context successfully can provide a great boost to your leadership effort, while failing in this arena can lead to the downfall of your project. But culture is never a neutral element. We all come to work with our humanity, and that will always be part of our process.

We want to help you create a plan that is as concrete and practical as possible. Take a few moments and think of a stakeholder group you are working with, or will be working with, that has a culture different from your own. Consider the four areas of cultural savvy we discussed in this chapter as you develop your plan.

- How is the group's culture different from yours in these categories?
- Where along the spectrum would you place this group for characteristics in each of the categories? For example, where would it fall on the spectrum of direct and indirect communication? Where would you place your culture in comparison?
- What skills and strategies offered in this chapter do you plan to use in your approach with this group?
- How will you adapt to the group and demonstrate your cultural savvy?

## A FINAL WORD ON DEMONSTRATING CULTURAL SAVVY

In a global matrix, interacting with different cultures is almost a daily occurrence. Whether you are in a global role interacting with colleagues from around the world or simply collaborating with people in different parts of your business, you need to be able to demonstrate cultural savvy. Attention to this leadership dimension is not a "nice to do" in the global matrix, it is a "must do well" part of successful matrix leadership.

CHAPTER 10

❖

# Coaching and Providing Feedback to Others

IN THE FIRST nine chapters of this book, our focus has been on helping you become a better matrix leader so you can optimize your performance and impact your organization. All the skills and strategies we've offered have revolved around helping you. In this chapter, we want to focus on how *you* can help *others*.

Whether you are leading a team and are invested in them improving their matrix leadership skills or are committed to supporting a colleague, providing effective feedback and coaching is an important skill for any matrix leader. As we have reiterated throughout the book, matrix skills are simple but not easy. They don't require a 160 IQ to apply—and, in fact, we have boiled them down to ensure they are straightforward to implement—however, they usually require practice and refinement before they are second nature, as they often mean we have to work against our deeply ingrained mental and behavioral habits.

When working in a matrix environment, it is hard to see ourselves in action. We can't always know how we impact others. Like other high-level abilities, matrix leadership skills take time to master. All leaders need to practice these skills and get quality feedback to understand how their efforts are manifesting and being perceived by the matrix world. This is where you can help others. Whether the other person is a member of your team or a colleague, they will most likely not master the matrix quickly and could benefit from some coaching and feedback to make adjustments or refine their approach. For all of these reasons, it is vital that you focus not only on improving your own matrix skills but on helping others around you.

## CREATING ACCOUNTABILITY

One extremely beneficial aspect of establishing a coaching relationship is the inherent level of accountability it creates. In the world of training and development, a hot-button topic for many years concerns the most effective techniques to sustain learning. With all the research that has been done, the element that continues to be near the top of the list boils down to a simple word: accountability.

The reality is this: When we need to acquire a new skill, it is usually because our current approach and the deeply ingrained habits we have established over the years are no longer working well. As we've discussed, learning new behaviors isn't easy, and when they are challenged by old habits, we may need to get out of our comfort zone. Ultimately, this means we must be committed enough to diligently practice a new behavior (which requires effort and concentration). As we've discussed throughout, you must do this to improve your own skills, but if you are committed and show a sincere level of interest in helping others, you can make a world of a difference in the organization by coaching colleagues and teammates. Knowing that you are paying attention, observing, and even evaluating them in their progress, which they will discuss with you on a regular basis, dramatically increases the likelihood that those you coach will stay motivated and prioritize time to hone their leadership skills. You can help them be accountable.

## TRUE FEEDBACK AND COACHING FOR MATRIX LEADERSHIP SKILLS

Many leaders we have worked with feel that they are good at coaching others and providing feedback simply because of the coaching they do.

Although the fact that they do it is a good start, simply going through the motions is usually not enough. As with any other skill, coaching can be done in a way that makes it more or less effective.

## The Number-One Feedback Mistake

Many of you may have taken classes and read books about coaching and feedback. Virtually all of the leaders we work with have as well. However, the hard truth is that the majority of these leaders are not nearly as effective as they might assume when it comes to providing actionable feedback and coaching to enhance specific matrix leadership skills.

This is not an indictment of these leaders or a question of their commitment. As is common with matrix leadership skills, simply having taken coaching and feedback courses in the past does not mean you are equipped to successfully hold coaching discussions related to these skills. Perhaps you are one of the few who does this well; however, offering constructive feedback is a challenge for even the best-intentioned leaders because coaching matrix leadership skills requires tremendous nuance and proficiency. Since this is not a book on feedback or coaching, we will assume that you already possess the core coaching skills (i.e., asking questions to gain the other person's perspective and buy-in, ensuring that the person feels heard and the conversation is two-way, using effective language to minimize resistance, and generating motivation). We will keep our advice focused on areas where we have witnessed leaders, even those with advanced training in coaching, struggle.

Although the orientation of the skills below and the examples provided involve a leader imparting feedback to a team member, the same skills apply if you are giving feedback to a peer or even to your leader. Whatever your role or level in a matrix, these strategies will make you better at offering feedback and coaching.

The most common derailer is providing feedback that remains at the conceptual level:

- "It is critical that you step up your thought leadership in meetings. Right now you are too low impact."

- "Now that we are collaborating across boundaries, I really need you to prioritize strategic relationship building."
- "I found you to be a little too aggressive in today's meeting. It's key to find the right balance. I need you to be assertive and confident in advocating for our position, but we need to strike a collaborative tone as well."
- "I need you to do a better job of reading the audience in the meeting. You missed some important cues. Please make it a priority to get better at reading your impact."
- "Building trust is essential to our success in this partnership. I've heard complaints of some transparency issues on our end; let's make sure that doesn't continue in the future."
- "I need you to improve your influencing skills; you are not effectively bringing your stakeholders with you."
- "You have too narrow a focus and are perceived as a functional expert; I need to see more of an enterprise-wide perspective."

We could easily populate the remainder of this chapter with further examples of these types of coaching and feedback discussions. As well-meaning as they may be, such statements are generally not very helpful. Why? They do not provide the specific, behavioral descriptions that allow the recipient to clearly understand the nuanced *action* (or lack thereof) under discussion. You need to provide the kind of information that empowers those on the receiving end of the feedback to understand what they need to do differently. This is easier said than done, precisely because so many of the behaviors required of leaders in the matrix are subtle and highly nuanced.

### "Camera-Check" Feedback

The trick to providing useful, action-oriented comments is employing what we call *camera-check feedback*. The criterion for delivering camera-check feedback is ensuring that the feedback you are providing is so behaviorally specific that a video camera could observe what you are describing.

We can likely agree that, while the feedback offered in the previous section is descriptive on a broader level, it does not clarify for the recipient the precise behavior that needs to be adjusted. Camera-check feedback solves this problem by:

1. Including a specific date and time the behavior needing development occurred
2. Describing the behavior as if a video camera were seeing and hearing it
3. Outlining the impact of the behavior

Below we will show the camera-check alternative to contrast with the conceptual feedback examples above. As you read, the benefits of the camera check are readily apparent.

**Conceptual feedback:** "It is critical that you step up your thought leadership in these meetings. Right now you are too low impact."

**Camera-check feedback:** "I was struck during the meeting this morning that when the topic of efficiencies came up, you didn't weigh in. I know from several one-on-one conversations we have had that you have strong opinions on the topic and, I believe, could influence the group to go in a better direction. Going forward, please ensure that you offer your perspective on this topic. This is how we will raise our impact."

**Conceptual feedback:** "Now that we are collaborating across boundaries, I really need you to prioritize strategic relationship building."

**Camera-check feedback:** "Now that we are collaborating with stakeholder groups beyond our function, it is essential that we strengthen our relationships among them. Please do an analysis of your current relationships with these new stakeholder groups and then let's schedule thirty minutes next week to review where you are today and identify a plan to strengthen your connection going forward."

**Conceptual feedback:** "I found you to be a little too aggressive in today's meeting. It's key we find the right balance. I need you to be assertive and confident in advocating for our position, but we need to strike a collaborative tone as well."

**Camera-check feedback:** "The qualities I really value in you are your confidence and the way you advocate for our team. What I noticed in the meeting with sales today is that there is an opportunity to refine that strength to ensure your intention matches your impact. Specifically, at the conclusion of your presentation when you were sharing your recommendations, you used the phrase, 'As you can see, based on the data, this is the only way to go.' Then, when Ingrid challenged your premise, your response was, 'Ingrid, I appreciate your concern, but this really is a no-brainer.' I'm concerned the team may have felt that language was more 'commanding' rather than collaborative. I have alternative phrases I can share with you that will allow you to achieve both clarity and confidence while still being collaborative."

**Conceptual feedback:** "I need you to do a better job of reading the audience in the meeting. You missed some important cues. Please make it a priority to get better at reading your impact."

**Camera-check feedback:** "You may not have been aware, but when you made the comment about cutting head count, Pierre noticeably shifted in his chair, leaned back, and folded his arms. And after that comment, he stopped making eye contact with you and did not speak for the remainder of the meeting. Pierre is a key decision maker, and it's critical to pick up on those kinds of cues of concern or hesitation. I'd like to work with you to develop a plan to improve your ability to spot these types of reactions, including how to respond to them skillfully."

**Conceptual feedback:** "Building trust is essential to our success in this partnership. I've heard complaints of some transparency issues on our end; let's make sure that doesn't continue in the future."

**Camera-check feedback:** "It may not have been your intention, but when you decided not to share the latest consumer data with our business partners until the meeting began—even though you had it for over a week—they felt you were withholding important information. Going forward, let's pay extra attention to being mindful of who expects to see the data and let's share it in a timely fashion to build trust with them."

**Conceptual feedback:** "I need you to improve your influencing skills; you are not effectively bringing your stakeholders with you."

**Camera-check feedback:** "As you know, our ability to gain buy-in from our stakeholders is key, since they can decide whether or not to implement our proposed system. I noticed during your presentation that the compelling reasons you provided were exclusively focused on their impact to the global strategy. However, you didn't lean in to any particular benefits related to their markets, nor did you reference any information that originated directly from their market. I received feedback from the group that they believe you are only concerned about global needs, not theirs. I have some strategies I'd like to share to help you increase your ability to bring these stakeholders along."

**Conceptual feedback:** "You have too narrow a focus; I need to see more of an enterprise-wide perspective."

**Camera-check feedback:** "I have noticed that in the last three meetings we have been in together with supply chain, you have shared only technical legal advice without demonstrating a broader perspective of the impact on their world. Our role as the legal team has evolved. We have to go beyond offering purely legal advice. In order to have a seat at the table, we have to take steps to increase our understanding, both of the business and the functions we support. This will enable us to offer our legal recommendations while demonstrating that we understand the realities they are dealing with on the ground."

Now that you have a number of examples to draw from, we hope you see some clear improvements over purely conceptual feedback. Camera-check feedback gives the recipients a sharper understanding of why their current behavior is ineffective from a matrix leadership perspective. This is really significant. We have endless examples of clients we have coached who, when we ask whether they know their development areas, can list them immediately. However, they then explain that, while they were given feedback that these were their development areas, they weren't completely clear what, specifically, they were doing that was getting in the way. So, of course, they didn't know what to do differently. They described attempts to address these areas, but they often got feedback that they had not adequately improved. Again, we are not criticizing these managers; it is challenging to provide feedback and coaching for such complex matrix leadership skills. However, when you are able to offer specific advice that shows feedback recipients how to change their behavior, you will be in a position to take your coaching to the next level.

Another benefit of camera-check feedback is that the solution to the performance issue is sometimes contained right in the feedback. For instance, in the example above regarding the person who did not weigh in during meetings, even when the topic under discussion was an area of expertise, the advice speaks for itself. Often, though, the skill development plan is more detailed and requires further coaching. Even in scenarios where further skill development is required, the camera-check examples set up a clear picture of the behavior that needs to be improved.

Providing feedback in this way also tends to reduce defensiveness. You are not labeling this individual as too aggressive; you are simply pointing out how some of his phrasing may land on people. For the most part, it is much easier for people to hear how others are reacting to their behavior than to accept a label they may feel is unfair.

Finally, it is difficult to argue with camera-check feedback. After all, it is a detailed, objective, behavioral description that is modeled on realistic image capture. It's hard to argue with a camera. On the other hand, if you provide feedback such as, "I need you to be a more proactive collaborator" or "You need to be more open-minded," you leave a lot of room for rebuttal.

Think of a team member, peer, or more senior leader you believe has an opportunity area in the matrix leadership arena. Create a camera-check feedback message for that person. Remember, the criteria are:

1. Providing a specific date and time the behavior needing development occurred
2. Describing the behavior in a way that is so specific a video camera could see and hear it
3. Outlining the impact the behavior has

## DEVELOPING AN ACTION PLAN
## FOR YOUR MENTEE

Whether you are coaching or providing feedback to a team member, someone you are mentoring, or a peer who is an accountability buddy (covered later in the chapter), helping the person devise an action plan can be an extremely valuable exercise. The action plan should outline the skill to be acquired by the person, the structure that supports the skill acquisition (a training program, mentoring sessions, etc.), and the detailed framework that ensures the team member has the encouragement and ongoing guidance needed to reach his or her development goals.

So often, we see well-intentioned leaders go to great lengths to provide coaching and feedback, but they do not take the next step to help the person build an action plan. On some occasions, feedback and a few tips are enough, but most of the time that doesn't cut it, especially with matrix skills. Influencing without authority, becoming more strategic, and developing executive presence are not easy abilities to cultivate. These skills require a strong plan—and the most important goal is ensuring that the leader learns the skills and develops the insights she needs to succeed. There are a number of learning options:

- training courses
- peer coaching
- shadowing a person who excels in the area
- executive coaching
- university programs
- coaching and/or teaching by you

The more flexibility the person has in choosing the specific action plan, the more likely she will be to buy in. That said, you need to have confidence that the approach has a high likelihood for success. Once you have determined the best route, agree on clear dates for when the steps will be executed. One powerful way to develop these kinds of plans is as part of your formal performance-review process. With some of our clients, reviews occur biannually, while others have them quarterly. By making the development area and development plan part of this process, you can ensure that it will remain top of mind. As importantly, by including the action plan and creating these mutual agreements, you will ensure that *you* stay on track as a coach and minimize the likelihood of becoming distracted or drifting on your commitments.

## Inspect What You Expect

"Inspect what you expect" simply means that you systematically check in to monitor the individual's progress against the goals set in the action plan. This may be the single most common omission from the coaching process. And, with our objective of supporting sustained learning, it may also be the most important.

Check-ins are a powerful step of the coaching process for many reasons. First, they show that you care and that the person's progress really matters to you. It's great to have a rousing feedback discussion with a team member about why it is so important for him to develop his advanced communication skills, but if you don't follow up for the next six months, the message is clear—it didn't really matter that much. This can cause the person you are coaching to lose motivation. On the other hand, it can really light a fire to agree upon a series of specific times when you will be discussing how the action plan is progressing. Not only do these meetings remind the person that he will need to share the progress he has made, they are also motivating because they show him that you care enough to follow up and observe and support his learning. This level of accountability is a significant catalyst in getting people to prioritize the skill development they need.

Here's an example: Let's say you were working with one of your team members, Ksenia, to improve her executive presence and meeting impact. You skillfully delivered your camera-check feedback to demonstrate her underparticipation and tentativeness, and she is now committed to learning. You developed an action plan together, which included Ksenia signing up for a course on executive presence that would be conducted in three weeks. To "inspect what you expect," you might say to her:

> Ksenia, this is great. I appreciate your openness to learning, and I think we have a good plan to help you gain the skills you need to improve. In order to support your success, I would like for us to choose one meeting per month that we both agree is the type of meeting where your contribution and impact are critical. After each meeting, you and I will take twenty minutes to discuss how the meeting went, so we can take full advantage of the learning opportunity while it is fresh in both our minds. I'm going to ask you to lead the discussion when we meet and would like you to arrive having reflected on the following three areas:
>
> 1.  How did you prepare for the meeting?
>
> 2.  What was your strategy and game plan?
>
> 3.  How would you evaluate what worked well and what did you find to be difficult?
>
> The purpose is twofold. First, let's capture your successes so you can replicate them in the future. Second, as this is a learning

process, we can discuss anything that still felt difficult and brainstorm a solution for the future.

Hopefully, your positive intent comes through in your tone and language. This is not about you micromanaging or looking over your team member's shoulder to catch her making a mistake; this is about providing ongoing support.

Finally, it is important to "catch people doing things right." Remember that, for those who commit the time, energy, and concentration to learning and demonstrating a new behavior or skill, the task is not easy. And it can be quite disheartening to put in all that effort and execute successfully, only to have your success go unacknowledged. Remember to provide positive feedback when you observe effort and improvement. This is not only highly motivating, it is a powerful factor in reinforcing the right behavior.

To gain that second benefit, make sure you provide your positive feedback in camera-check style. It's one thing to say something like, "Great job in the meeting today!" It's another to say, "Ksenia, your presence and impact in this morning's meeting were excellent. I noticed that you got into the discussion within the first five minutes, gave your ideas clearly, used confident language, and even gracefully and calmly reinserted yourself into the discussion when Sebastian interrupted you. Ksenia, those types of behaviors are really transforming the way you are showing up." As you can see, not only will this feedback land with significantly more meaning and credibility, it also reinforces the specific behaviors you want to see her exhibit in the future.

## Accountability Partners

Another effective way to help drive positive sustainability is by finding an accountability partner for the individual you are coaching. You may certainly serve as an accountability partner, though your commitments as a leader may mean you do not have the requisite time to devote on a day-to-day basis. If your other obligations prevent you from being involved in frequent check-ins, another accountability partner could be the answer; the partner may be someone else on the person's team or someone outside the department. It could even be someone in her personal life. The idea is that the person feels there is someone who will be watching and keeping tabs on her progress. This will keep her motivated and focused. People are more likely to follow through when they make a promise or commitment to someone else. It's like going to the gym; if you promised a friend you would meet her there, you are more likely to go than if you were going alone.

Here are some tips to help your mentee set up an accountability partnership:

1. Ask the person to find someone she trusts and respects. Sometimes someone outside of her team/function is a good option. As we mentioned, you may serve as an accountability partner, depending upon your time and other commitments.
2. The accountability partner must understand the team member's development areas and why they are important, and the partner must recognize the specific actions the team member needs to meet the goals.
3. The accountability partner and team member should set up regular check-in times to discuss progress (these can be via text messages, phone calls, emails).
4. The goals and strategies must be recalibrated regularly based on feedback during performance reviews.

## THE PINNACLE: CREATING A FEEDBACK-RICH CULTURE

One of the central guiding principles and aspirations of an integrated structure is leveraging diversity of thought and perspective. This principle is based on the understanding that there is no way any individual can see as much as the group can; each person is limited by her expertise, experience, and thought patterns.

One of the great ways to benefit from this concept is by creating a feedback-rich culture on your team. A feedback-rich culture is one in which feedback—both corrective and positive—flows freely, is expected, and, most of all, is genuinely seen as a positive. It is not something to be afraid of.

Here is the reality: your team members are often in the best position to provide you (if you are leading this particular team) and one another feedback. Why? Very simply, they are constantly observing you in all the key situations where you are demonstrating (or failing to demonstrate) matrix leadership behaviors. They are in meetings with you and on conference calls. They also have networks that are likely to give them insight into how you are perceived. If you think we are exaggerating this, we invite you to do a thought experiment right now: If you are currently working on a team that has been together a minimum of six months, select three team members (if you have more time, feel free to choose more). Now, imagine that you were scheduled to have a confidential call with an executive coach to provide your feedback for each team member's strengths and development opportunities. Would you be able to offer some valuable insights regarding these three team members?

We're guessing that answer is yes. The reason we can make that guess with high certainty is that we have been the executive coaches on thousands of calls exactly like the one we described above. And, assuming team members have worked together for six months or more, we have never received the following response when asking for feedback: "Actually, I have no idea or point of view on Enrique's strengths or development areas. Yes, we've worked on the same team for nine months now, but so far I have just not formed any opinions or heard anything about how he is thought of outside of our team."

This has never happened! In fact, team members know each other very well and have a wealth of valuable insights they could share with each other. We get that we are probably reminding you of something you already know. So, why don't teams more frequently share this extremely valuable information and feedback? Because it is difficult. Providing feedback to those who do not report to you and, in particular, giving feedback "up" is challenging because of the fear of a negative reaction, tension, conflict, and even potentially being punished for it. However, teams that are able to establish a feedback-rich culture can really accelerate learning and, ultimately, effectiveness.

In our experience, the teams that achieve and sustain this high aspiration usually have a team leader who makes constructive feedback a top priority and authentically "walks the talk." Frankly, most leaders we know will give their teams a speech when they first begin working together. It goes something like this: "I want you all to know that I am counting on you to give me your feedback and challenge me. I don't have all the answers and I have blind spots—I am counting on your insights to help me be the best leader I can be. Don't hold back. Hit me between the eyes. I also hope we can all provide each other feedback. After all, feedback is the breakfast of champions!"

Sounds great. However, that speech is not always followed up with *behavior* that creates the safe environment in which helpful feedback flows. In fact, many leaders who have given a speech along these lines then engage in behavior that conflicts with their stated goal; they dismiss feedback, shut down people who challenge them, and marginalize team members who give corrective feedback. That creates a chilling effect, and no team member feels safe to share their critiques. Leaders who are successful in creating a feedback-rich culture know that the speech is the easy part. There are a number of systems, processes, and behaviors that need to follow to bring that culture to life. It's not just about giving a nice speech.

There are two main hurdles to achieving a true feedback-rich culture. The first is overcoming the fear of negative reactions from others and making feedback a positive experience. The second is transforming feedback from something that happens rarely and generally only when there is a "problem," which contributes to the stigma around it, to an experience that is normalized, routine, and expected.

## Minimizing the Difficulty of Providing and Receiving Feedback

When it comes to feedback, we prefer realism over concept. In theory, the notion that we could all benefit by giving each other developmental feedback is obvious. In reality, from an emotional standpoint, it is difficult to do. Even giving developmental feedback to someone who reports directly to you is uncomfortable for most. Generally, it is not pleasant to deal with defensiveness and negative reactions. That fear is exponentially higher when providing corrective feedback to a peer. There's a risk that the response will be something along the lines of, "Last I checked, I don't report to you," or "If I want feedback from you, I'll ask," or "You are confusing me with someone who cares," and that the outcome will be a strained relationship or a full-blown vicious cycle, which can be overwhelming.

The bottom line is that the majority of folks will weigh the pros and cons and come to the following conclusion: "That's the second time I've seen Simon communicate in a way that is shutting down the conversation. It would probably benefit him to understand that. However, he seems like a pretty aggressive guy. He could take it the wrong way and end up upset with me. It's not worth it."

Giving feedback "up" can be even more daunting. "What if she gets upset and holds a grudge? She can retaliate by lowering my ratings or not supporting my hopes for promotion. That's way too big a risk."

The most direct way to combat this type of disposition is by outlining general expectations regarding feedback and then modeling a gracious response when someone provides you with corrective feedback. Imagine that a peer or someone who reports to you musters up the courage to offer corrective feedback to you. If you listen intently and then respond, "Eliana, I can't thank you enough for providing me this feedback. It was a total blind spot for me and I can see how it was impacting my effectiveness. I'm putting together a plan to correct that immediately. Please, if you notice other behaviors you think may be hindering my success don't hesitate to tell me." Do you suppose that person will be inclined to provide feedback in the future if the need arose? Do you suppose she will share your response with others, and she will choose to respond graciously herself if you or others find the need to provide her with feedback in the future? Hopefully the answer is yes.

The key, then, is to react in an open and constructive way when someone you do not report to (in fact, the person may report to you!) provides you with corrective feedback. Simple . . . but not easy. There is a reason most people have a negative association with receiving corrective feedback. It is very easy to get defensive. We are human beings. We have egos. When someone provides us with input that contradicts our self-image and bruises our ego, our natural instinct is to defend ourselves. These feelings can increase exponentially if we don't think it is "someone's place"—they are not your direct supervisor—meaning a peer or someone more junior in the org chart. This does not make you a bad person, it makes you a human being. If we can accept that reality, we now have the opportunity to *intentionally* cultivate our capacity to receive feedback skillfully. Now, let's get into the how-to of this important ability, so you can model it effectively and provide valuable tips on giving and receiving feedback as you coach your team members.

### Cultivate the Right Mindset

Practice self-talk that affirms that feedback is not only inevitable, it is also extremely beneficial. When you intentionally cultivate this orientation, you will not be surprised by feedback when you receive it, and you will begin to seek it and consider it a positive. The best way to develop this disposition is with an intentional practice of self-talk. Below are some self-talk phrases that, with enough repetition, will help get you there:

- "Everyone has blind spots, and that includes me."
- "It is impossible to accurately predict how I am perceived by others. I count on feedback to ensure my intentions match my impact."
- "Feedback is the key to my ongoing growth and development."

- "Feedback is a gift."
- "Feedback is kind of like spinach—it may not taste great, but it is really good for me!"

## Center Yourself

Receiving feedback that contradicts your self-image can be emotionally jarring, and protective instincts can quickly rise to the surface. If left unchecked, defensive behavior can shut down feedback in the future. We encourage you to find a place to sit and continue the conversation (if you are not already). Remind yourself to take a few deep breaths to calm yourself, and remain poised.

## Listen with Curiosity and Empathy

One of the best ways to demonstrate your sincere interest in the feedback and put the provider at ease is to ask some open questions. Simultaneously, you will gain a deeper understanding of the feedback itself.

- "Wow, that is really valuable feedback I wasn't aware of. Can you describe that behavior in more detail? I want to make sure I have a full understanding."
- "I had no idea that there was a perception that I wasn't open-minded. That is definitely something I want to address. Can you give me some examples of when that occurred?"
- "It's hard to hear that I had that impact on the team. It wasn't my intention and I'm committed to learning how not to repeat that in the future."

## Show Appreciation

Assuming your gratitude is genuine, this is perhaps the single most important step in creating a positive experience for someone giving you feedback. Remember, the other person fears that you are going to react negatively and be upset that she brought this feedback to your attention.

Even if you do not agree with the feedback, you should still thank the other person for providing it.

- "I am really grateful that you brought this to my attention. I would have likely continued the same behavior not knowing it was hurting my reputation."
- "I know it's not easy giving feedback to a peer; that really took courage. Thank you."

### Evaluate the Feedback

Just because someone provides you with feedback does not mean he is automatically correct in his assessment. It is possible that the person has limited information, doesn't have the full context, or, simply, has a genuinely different interpretation of the situation than you do. The key reflection point is to be as objective as possible when evaluating the feedback. On the other hand, if we are too open to the feedback and act on every piece we receive, we risk being whipsawed. Below are a few reflection questions to ask yourself to help you discern intelligently:

- **What does the feedback tell me about this person or my impact on her?** At a minimum, this feedback is giving you valuable information about how you are impacting this person. Even if you ultimately don't agree with her assessment as general truth, you could still decide to shift your behavior with her specifically.
- **Does this sound familiar?** If you have heard this type of feedback before, and disregarded it the last couple of times . . . it may be time to take it seriously!
- **Could this feedback be generalized?** Even if you haven't heard this specific feedback before, as you listen to the examples the person offers, can you connect how he (or others) could have that impression of you or interpret your behavior in this way, even if it is not your intention? If the answer is yes, you may want to accept the feedback and act on it.

If, after thorough and honest reflection, you truly disagree with the feedback another person is providing you, it is still important to thank the person and handle the conversation the right way to create a positive experience. For instance:

> Christopher, thank you again for taking the time to provide me with this feedback. As you provided examples, I can definitely see why you are concerned about my behavior in meetings being too assertive from your perspective. As I reflect on this, I want to share with you why I have a slightly different view on it. Based on my past experience working with this stakeholder group, they are quite aggressive in their communication and will easily dominate the meeting if you let them. This is why I have taken the direct and assertive approach you describe. I am concerned that if I didn't, the other group will dictate the meeting agenda and decisions, and that would be a bigger risk to us. That said, I am happy to get some additional feedback from other team members to see if they share your concern and will respond accordingly.

### Learn and Change

Make a commitment to the person and yourself about the action steps you are going to take to make a change. A powerful trust-building accountability technique is to ask this person if he would do you the favor of following up and giving you feedback again if he doesn't see a change in this behavior in the future.

### Recognize Feedback with Your Team

This step is really important, as it relates to the goal of creating a feedback-rich culture on the team. If a peer or direct report has provided you with valuable feedback that helped you improve, thank her for it publicly, in front of the rest of the team. This practice not only feels great to the person you are praising, it sends a powerful signal to the entire team reinforcing the value of feedback.

## Making Feedback Normal, Routine, and Expected

The final step in ensuring a strong feedback-rich culture is simple but very important: implement specific processes and systems that require feedback conversations to happen more frequently and consistently. In this way, feedback becomes normal rather than a scary experience. We recently worked with a leader who did an excellent job of incorporating this and the other key strategies.

Samuel, the president and CEO of a regional branch office of a health care company, was looking to institute a rapid and successful on-boarding process and build a strong and highly functioning team. He had been promoted to the role less than six months earlier, and the organization as a whole, including his branch, was undergoing considerable change.

The organization was moving toward a more integrated structure, which meant a considerable shift in ways of working going forward. In addition to core leadership and team start-up essentials (i.e., conveying his vision and leadership style, building trust and cohesion among his team, building alignment around top priorities, etc.), the key to Samuel and his leadership team's success was an ability to quickly develop the insights and skills necessary to lead in the new organizational structure. By exemplifying these skills themselves, they would have the credibility and understanding to lead their entire organization through change.

One of Samuel's mantras was: "We need to be the change we want to see in our organization." And he recognized that if he and his group could cultivate a feedback-rich team, they could dramatically accelerate their individual and collective learning curve, all while creating a powerful sense of trust and purpose.

To bring his plan to life, Samuel partnered with the learning and development (L&D), talent, and HR partners to roll out the newly identified leadership competencies. To complement these competencies, they brought in external experts to facilitate self-awareness and skill sessions to equip Samuel and the team with the critical skills and tools they needed to successfully achieve their goals. At this stage, Samuel really began to put his feedback-rich team to work.

1. **Developing individual action plans:** Once the training was complete, Samuel asked each of his team members to choose one or two specific skill areas to focus on; they were to choose the skills they believed would have the biggest impact on their ability to lead successfully in the new org structure. He would review the action plans in each of his upcoming one-on-one meetings over the following two weeks.

2. **Sharing of individual action plans:** Once all the team members had settled on their development plans, Samuel asked them to share their one or two action-plan items with the entire group at their upcoming team meeting. Samuel led the effort by first sharing his action plan with the group. He introduced the team exercise in the following way:

   > With our goal of being the most effective team we can be, and to help lead our organization through all of these change initiatives, I firmly believe we are our own best resource, advocates, and coaches. There is so much talent and experience on this team, and I want us to fully tap into it. In that spirit, I would like to share with you my action plan and my development focus for the next six months. I invite you to provide me with feedback on how I can continue to improve during our designated one-on-one meetings.

   As a result of his openness and his willingness to share his development needs and action plan, Samuel set a tone of learning and transparency, creating a safe space for his team. Taking his lead, the rest of his team shared their action plans with the group as well.

3. **Accountability partners:** Once the group had shared their action plans, each team member selected an accountability partner on the team. They set up a standard monthly meeting (often a lunch or coffee), where they shared their implementation of the action plans with each other and gave feedback about progress and challenges. In addition, they were asked to provide each

other with "spot" coaching on a spontaneous basis whenever one observed her accountability partner successfully executing against one of the action-plan items or if she saw an opportunity for improvement. The accountability partners also committed to making themselves available if their partners wanted support or to brainstorm a specific scenario for their action plans.

4. On a quarterly basis, the partners agreed that they would share highlights of their action plans, progress, and learnings with the entire team for the purposes of learning.

As Samuel's executive coach and accountability partner, part of our process was to ensure that the feedback was current and that we conducted interviews with his team members two months into the coaching to get real-time reactions on how they had progressed. The feedback from his team was consistent, with comments including:

"We really appreciate Samuel's openness and vulnerability with us; sharing his action plan and what he is working on created a safe space for us to share our challenge areas without it being a negative."

"It's been so great working as a team to help ourselves improve. The truth is, our organization has never been really good at feedback. I've received more actionable feedback in the last two months than I have in five years!"

"With this new system I can't hide or procrastinate on my development areas like I have in the past. It's not easy, but I am already seeing improvements."

## CREATING YOUR COACHING AND FEEDBACK ACTION PLAN

Coaching your team members and creating a feedback-rich culture on your team is hard work. It means challenging yourself and getting out of your comfort zone—and encouraging others to do so as well. It takes courage and persistence. Many leaders talk about how they aspire to "radical candor" on their teams, with feedback and coaching

---

### YOUR MATRIX MOMENT: PROVIDING COACHING AND FEEDBACK

- A critical aspect of matrix leadership is contributing to the development of leadership skills in others through effective coaching and feedback.
- A key part of giving feedback successfully is making the advice concrete rather than conceptual. Remember to use camera-check feedback—your comments should be so behaviorally specific that a video camera could record the actions you are describing.
- The ultimate goal is to create a feedback-rich culture that leverages the insights of the team through consistent, free-flowing, constructive critiques.

---

flowing freely, but few follow through. Going beyond the buzzwords and inaugurating an open environment requires a high level of commitment, but it can be done. Take time now to plan your coaching and feedback strategies.

1. Identify team members, peers, or even senior leaders who might benefit if you share your insights with them. For people who report to you, you have a coaching responsibility; others in your organization may also value your constructive advice.
2. What kind of language will you use to communicate your feedback? Think back to what you read in this chapter and the examples provided. If it helps, write your feedback on paper.
3. How will you model gracious acceptance of feedback for your team?
4. What key elements do you plan to include in the action plan of team members you are coaching? What supports will you offer?

# A FINAL WORD ON COACHING
# AND FEEDBACK

As a matrix leader, one of the most impactful roles you can play is that of coach to others as they develop their matrix leadership skills. However, coaching your team effectively on matrix skills requires a high level of proficiency. Cultivating a culture in which feedback is truly appreciated—given and received with grace and gratitude—is also a valuable goal. With the guidance offered in this chapter, you will not only be able to help others improve in their jobs and further their careers, you will also help turn your organization into one that prizes feedback. Moreover, you are displaying your value within the organization and helping to enhance your brand. This is a true win-win for both yourself and your organization.

# Conclusion

GIVEN ALL THE information, tips, and strategies we have provided throughout this book, we'd like to circle back to our core focus when we began: building a bridge between a conceptual understanding of matrix leadership skills and practical plans for implementing them in a way that invites greater success. It is our singular hope that, as a result of reading this book, you have gained some specific, tangible knowledge that you can apply and that will increase your effectiveness in your organization as well as help your career.

Because of our focus on this outcome, we have been continuously encouraging you to reflect, create action plans, and concentrate on the importance of scheduling time to execute those plans. If the message seemed repetitive at times, that was by design. As busy as we all are, we get easily distracted unless our important tasks are on the calendar.

All of this said, we know that becoming a masterful matrix leader is a journey, not a destination. Please do not expect that you will immediately go back into your workplace with a perfect command of all these skills. You will not only overwhelm yourself with such a broad task, you will predictably set yourself up for frustration and failure. Consider the mantra: "Progress, not perfection."

We also recommend taking a bite-sized-chunks approach to learning. Identify one or two learning areas that resonated with you most in the book and focus on only these for the next six months. Once you have developed confidence in them and they have become second nature, go back and select one or two more. Use the template below to plan and track your actions and to form a clear picture of what success will look like. The key is to be as specific as possible.

| Development Area | Actions To Be Taken | Measurement of Success |
|---|---|---|
| | | |
| | | |
| | | |

In the final chapter, on developing coaching and feedback skills, we discussed the power of accountability. Consider creating an accountability system for yourself. Certainly, you can always have a conversation with your direct supervisor, sharing the behaviors you intend to focus on and asking for periodic check-ins to gain feedback. This can be an extremely valuable exercise on multiple fronts. For one, it makes your personal investment in your ongoing leadership development visible to your leader. Being perceived as a self-starting learner is always a positive. In addition, you have now created a rich accountability loop that can help motivate you if you start to drift. Another option is finding an accountability partner who can help you stay on track; we strongly recommend you consider this as you move forward with your own development action plan.

We would like to conclude with an element of the personal. One of our favorite parts of teaching these skills to leaders is that so many have applications beyond our work settings, spilling over into our personal lives. The skills, insights, and strategies presented in this book will not only make you a better matrix leader, they will make you a better friend, sibling, parent, and life partner. If you commit to cultivating a positive overall mindset, you will stretch yourself in many empowering ways. You will increase your capacity for empathy, putting yourself in others' shoes and seeing things through their eyes. You will increase your curiosity, patience, and listening skills. You will also become a more collaborative and effective communicator. The power of deep collaboration can be even more meaningful with our loved ones than with our stakeholders.

# Acknowledgments

W<small>E WOULD LIKE TO</small> thank all of the exceptional leaders and organizations we have had the privilege of working with around the globe. It is what we have learned from our work with them which has enabled the content of this book. Thank you.

We would also like to give a very special thanks to Alan Fuks, whose hard work was critical in bringing the book to life.

—John and Marty

# Index

# About the Authors

**John Futterknecht** is an Executive Coach who has had the privilege to engage one-on-one with over 500 global leaders since beginning his career in 1998. In addition, he has facilitated over one thousand leadership development programs at Fortune 500 companies across five continents and in more than twenty countries.

Over the course of his career, John's areas of specialization have continued to evolve along with his clients' needs. In recent years, his focus has been in the area he calls "Leadership for the Twenty-First Century," including topics like leading in Global Matrix structures, collaborating across boundaries, influencing without authority, and developing Resilience and Mental Toughness. Additionally, he has helped thousands of leaders demystify and demonstrate essential leadership attributes such as Executive Presence and Strategic Thinking. John's clients mostly appreciate his ability to tackle complex leadership capabilities and break them down into practical and behavioral skills and strategies.

John is the President and Co-Founder of Optimum Associates. He has earned an MEd in Adult Education and Training at Colorado State University.

**Dr. Marty Seldman** is a corporate trainer, executive coach, and organizational psychologist. He received a BA in mathematics from Cornell University and completed his PhD in clinical psychology at Temple University.

From 1972 to 1986, Marty specialized in the field of training. This experience included training trainers, designing training programs, and serving as VP of Sales for a training company.

In 1986 he began his career as an executive coach and has become the coach of choice for many Fortune 500 companies. Marty has trained tens of thousands of executives around the globe through his seminars and coached over 1,800 executives one-on-one. Approximately half of the executives Marty has coached are women, people of color, or non-US executives.

Marty has written several books, including *Survival of the Savvy* (Free Press, 2004), which was a *Wall Street Journal* bestseller; *Super Selling Through Self-Talk* (Price Stern Sloan, Inc., 1986); and *Customer Tells* (Kaplan Publishing, 2007), which is co-authored with John Futterknecht and Ben Sorensen.

In addition to Marty's corporate work, he is active in the non-profit sector as a coach and consultant. He also serves on the boards of four organizations that work in the areas of human rights and poverty alleviation.